WALK OF AGES

WALK OF AGES

A Generational Journey from
Mt. Whitney to Death Valley

WITHANEE ANDERSEN AND JIM ANDERSEN

UNIVERSITY OF NEVADA PRESS | *Reno & Las Vegas*

University of Nevada Press | Reno, Nevada 89557 USA
www.unpress.nevada.edu
Copyright © 2024 by University of Nevada Press
All rights reserved
Hiker graphics: page 1 © JanStopka, page 3 Yurii / Adobe Stock
Manufactured in the United States of America

FIRST PRINTING

Cover design by Caroline Dickens

LIBRARY OF CONGRESS CATALOGING-IN-PUBLICATION DATA ON FILE
ISBN 978-1-64779-106-3 (paper)
ISBN 978-1-64779-107-0 (ebook)
LCCN 2023942812

To my Daddy,
the light of my life, thank you for giving me this
and all of our adventures.
Your footsteps will always be too big to follow,
but I'll never quit trying. I love you.
Forever,
Your little girl

CONTENTS

ACKNOWLEDGMENTS

This book would never have been possible without a few folks propping me up along the way (which also happened on The Walk itself, I might add). Of course, my dad is and always will be the reason I ever find myself putting words on paper, and I never would have attempted this if he hadn't agreed to being my coauthor. At the time, I could have never understood how much these words we've written would come to mean to me. I am so grateful for our relationship—and the fact that we could always talk each other into anything, *obviously*. I love you dearly, Daddy.

My mom, who poured over these pages with us to keep us on track and grammatically correct (as much as possible). The most remarkable woman I know, she often pulls me up by my bootstraps to get me going again when I fall flat on my face, which I did several times during this process. Without her, Dad and I would have likely drank the beer but forgotten to write the book.

My big brother, Josh, whom I dare say may have even been the one to suggest we write a book about our adventure. I never thought of it until he planted that seed, but once he did, it's all I *ever* thought about. I remember him coming up with chapter titles while we ambled across the desert, taking my mind off the pain for a blissful micro-second.

My one-of-a-kind husband, Shawn. In this book process, he would always have me read the chapters aloud to him just like he had my dad do during The Walk. He'd howl with laughter or clap when I finished, making me feel like I was a Pulitzer winner. He also gave me the proposal of a lifetime on top of Mt. Whitney and the incredible memory of asking my dad's permission beforehand. Those two were always up to some sort of mischief—but this time was my favorite. I am forever grateful and in love.

Lastly, to all Sandwalkers, originals and second editions: Jim Andersen, Ken Oberg, Glenn Burnett, Gary Ivie, Withanee Andersen Milligan, Shawn Milligan, Josh Rudelbach. You are all certifiably nuts. And I love you for it.

INTRODUCTION

—*Jim*—

I don't personally care for introductions to books because it seems like the author is trying to make a long story short just prior to the start of a long story.

However, I do think the title of this book, *Walk of Ages*, needs a bit of explanation. I just happened to make this walk from Mt. Whitney to Death Valley after turning thirty years old. It had been on my mind for a few years before I found three other people who were receptive to it, and they just happened to be near thirty years old also.

My daughter, Withanee, was in her late twenties when she told me she also wanted to walk from Mt. Whitney to Death Valley when she turned thirty, and she asked if I'd write down how we went about it day by day. So I did, resulting in a short self-published book titled *Sometimes a Great Notion...isn't, so much.* For some reason I found it necessary to put an introduction in that book also, and wound it up saying; "The dumbest crow in the world wouldn't even consider taking that route, so why would my college-educated daughter?"

"Because," she replied, "That's what you did when you were thirty years old."

Well, yes, there's that. But I never went to college.

So there seems to be an emptiness inherent in us humans that strikes around that age. I'm certain now that emptiness is a hole in our being that can only be filled by God. Take from that what you will, but it certainly proved to be true in our case. You may have even noticed "Walk of Ages" rhymes with the gospel song "Rock of Ages."

Then there are the chapter divisions: Withanee's from the perspective of the walkers, while mine are remembrances of the support party's role. You could say their universe was up and down, while ours was back and forth. Just like in real life, both were necessary to make the thing work.

So may God bless every step you take, even those between Mt. Whitney and Death Valley.

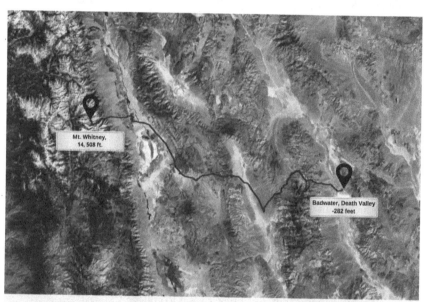

THE ROUTE OF THE SANDWALKERS: 1974, 2017

The route taken by Sandwalkers, past and present.

WHITNEY VERSUS WITHANEE

—Withanee—

September 25, 2017, 2 a.m.: A mere 5-ish hours after drifting off into a fitful sleep, I woke to my muffled cell phone alarm sounding somewhere deep in my sleeping bag. I sat up suddenly, frantically slapping around to find it.

FLAP! I hit the top of my bag, somewhere near my hip. Wait a minute, that can't be right.

FLAP!

I hit somewhere around the middle of my bag, my foggy brain starting to register something amiss in the inky darkness. I finally found my phone, silenced the alarm, and felt more curiously around the outside of my sleeping bag. The entire thing was...soggy. My blanket on top of my bag was wet. My hair was wet, and, as curly hair does, beginning to mat against my forehead. Even my pillow was soaked. Somehow, the entire inside of my tent was suspiciously wet.

"Awesome," I thought. "And this is how one stupid girl freezes to death on the way up Mt. Whitney."

I was trying to figure out how to put my socks on when I heard a loud engine roar to life, effectively breaking the peaceful silence of Lone Pine campground. Ahhh, that made me smile. My parents, who were also my support party for this insane endeavor, were not only awake but making me coffee by the obvious sound of the rental motor home generator. I still feel bad for waking up everyone in the campground at two in the morning, but not bad enough that I could have foregone coffee.

After putting on a couple layers while trying not to touch *any soaking thing* inside my tent, I unzipped the door and padded out into the darkness. I distinctly remember how bright the stars were and took a deliberate minute to look up toward the mountain I knew was looming over me yet couldn't see.

Well, this was it.

I had dragged everyone I truly loved down to this *danged* campground, to do this *ridiculous* feat that not many had done before me, and it all started today. Not able to comprehend the enormity of the week ahead of me, I zeroed in on the next 17 hours: up and back down Mt. Whitney. Piece of cake, right? My stomach turned. Our mission to walk from the highest point in the lower 48 to the lowest point in the western hemisphere sat sprawling in front of me, heckling. The feeling of foolishness settled in on me like one of the wet blankets inside my tent.

Could I do this?

Hiking Mt. Whitney was a feat unto itself without tacking on over 100 miles of relentless terrain after the fact. Both common sense and the stories my dad had captivated me with as a child told me that.

My dad.

They say that fathers and daughters have a special bond, but I always thought it was my dad and I that gave origin to that expression. My best friend from day one, I grew up always side by side with him. My childhood memories swell with pictures of my dad's smiling face: tree climbing, kite flying, water balloon fights, lying on our backs to find shapes in the clouds, endless adventures into the Nevada desert I grew up in.

As people grow older, the flame of wonder and intrigue that was there at infancy fades. My dad's never did. He sees the world so vastly different than anyone I have ever known, like it's just one big playground waiting to be discovered. This adventure was his idea more than forty years ago, and truth be told, he nearly died making it. Somewhere deep in the recesses of my childhood while I listened to his stories, a seed was planted. I later likened this to the seed of knowing God or the seed of reading the Bible, which later sprouted into beautiful things in my life.

My being here, now musing in the early morning darkness, was my way of honoring the man my world revolved around. My goal was to recreate his journey, if just to taste a tiny morsel of his past adventures and maybe find one of my own.

I took a deep breath and said a prayer to both God and Mt. Whitney (something like, "Please don't kill me, ole girl"). I knew what happened today would make or break this trip. If I couldn't make it to the highest point, then I couldn't even *start* my quest; an entire year of planning would be for nothing. Ah, well, best not to think too long on that—after all, I already had my socks on.

I picked my way over to the Minnie Winnie, tripping over a bush, muttering under my breath all the way, but lured by the promise of the loudest cup of coffee to have ever been brewed.

The next forty minutes or so is a dark blur in my memory, until all of a sudden, we were packed up and two sets of headlights wound their way up toward Whitney Portal: the four hikers in one car, the support party and all of the gear in Dad's trusty little red Toyota 4Runner. Anyone who owns a 4-cylinder vehicle understands the pain of a steep grade, so naturally we had a few minutes to spare after parking and hopping nimbly out of my big brother Josh's Subaru. The "nimbly" bit is something I remember because I didn't feel that way again for a long, long time. Anyway, this little gap in time gave my boyfriend, Shawn, and I a wonderfully sweet moment. We even saw a shooting star streak its way across the sky as we huddled together, totally in awe of what we were about to attempt. I suppose I should mention now that it was our third anniversary of dating, and as he helped me figure out how to lengthen my trekking pole (which should have been my first clue that I wasn't cut out for this), I was aware of how incredibly grateful I was that he was there.

The year we made The Walk, Shawn and I were both wildland firefighters for the US Forest Service; I was on an engine stationed out of Markleeville, California, and he worked for the Black Mountain Hotshots in Carson City, Nevada.

He was on his twelfth year in fire and had never asked for a day off because missing one day of work could mean missing the opportunity to be dispatched to a fire. Missing one fire assignment could mean missing two to three weeks of work with his crew, which translated to a pretty huge hit to his paycheck.

It was touch-and-go to see if he would even be granted the annual leave he requested, and he didn't confirm he was actually coming until two weeks prior to The Walk. That made me, with my type-A personality, nervous, because I am a planner through and through. Shawn is the opposite; he didn't even buy trekking poles! Actually, he didn't buy anything for the excursion except shoes, which he purchased just two days before we left for Lone Pine. I was totally flabbergasted at his nonchalance. Dad had told me time and time again how crucial a good shoe break-in was for this journey, and boy, did I take his advice seriously. I wore those expensive suckers everywhere I could. They felt nicely formed to my feet and I was genuinely worried about the condition Shawn's feet would be in at the end of this puppy. He wasn't concerned though, and isn't about most things. It's one of my favorite qualities about him.

Often referred to as "the hype man" in our friend circles, Shawn has an energy and cheerfulness that will turn a bleak situation into something else entirely. He can talk me up to do just about anything and, as somewhat of a pessimistic scaredy cat, I often need that. I couldn't have imagined doing this without him, and I would find myself tapping into his disposition more often than the beer cooler in the week ahead.

As for the other Second Edition Sandwalkers—my older brother, Josh, had been prepping for this day since I had told him about it more than a year prior. As a cerebral, just-in-case scenario kind of guy, he had all the gear *and more* that a backpacker could ever need.

He also had a little training. At forty, Josh was the oldest of any of the Sandwalkers—Original or Second Edition—but in great shape. He loves competing in Spartan Races, where crazy people run several miles and tackle obstacles for what they call "fun." He even talked me into doing one once, so I suppose this was my payback. I had to wade through several feet of mud between obstacles, *for crying out loud*.

My two brothers and I have a bit of an age gap, or maybe more of a canyon, as they are nine and eleven years older than I am. So really, he was old enough to know better than to attempt this but swore to come just to make sure I didn't quit. Man, does he know me well.

My other brother, Jed (whom I affectionately call Jeddy), was clearly smarter than the both of us and was happily sitting this one out.

The fourth member of our party was my good friend Kelly Harper. I had met her four years before when I was a scrawny and timid first-year wildland firefighter and she was my superior. I didn't have a whole lot of business signing up to fight wildfires, but I had applied anyway, to try to fulfill a 90-day "boots on the ground" requirement for a dispatcher position I was gunning for. At that point, I could only be a dispatcher on a seasonal basis. It was a job I enjoyed but couldn't make permanent until I had some experience in the field. It is an odd requirement, really, because most dispatchers aren't exactly in the shape necessary to be doing that sort of strenuous work. Evidently, I had gone about the whole thing backward because most dispatchers at these wildland centers *are* ex-firefighters whose bodies were simply too run down to continue with the physical demands of the job. Dispatch was the place where blown-out knees and bad backs abound, a very natural transition for those who had been bitten by the fire bug and couldn't bear to do anything else.

My entry into the fire world was more of a crash landing. I had recently lost fifty pounds (that I had put on working in dispatch and going to college, what a calorie-laden combo) and was, to put it mildly, somewhat less than tough. Self-conscious and scared senseless, I hadn't experienced one iota of physical labor in my twenty-four years. So, when I got the position on Engine 415 on the Humboldt-Toiyabe National Forest, I was so in over my head that it would have taken a sky hook by the belt loop to pull me out. To this day, I believe Kelly was that hook.

Before I had formally met Kelly, I was *terrified* of her. From the get-go, she was everything I knew I never would be: tough, fearless, adventurous, strong. I was beyond intimidated by her, so it was a pleasant surprise when she took me under her wing on my very first day of work in such a foreign environment. I distinctly remembered the first run I went on with all of my coworkers. The word *run* having never truly entered my vocabulary, she trailed way in the back with me muttering words of encouragement with each agonizing step. This was something she has never stopped doing, and she quickly became one of my favorite people I have ever had the chance to meet. We are polar opposites in many ways, especially when it comes to politics, but somehow I am just a magnet to that girl. And, as it turned out, I was right about her being all tough and strong, but she is also a whole lot of other adjectives: hilarious, sweet, incredibly kind, smart, self-assured, supportive, loyal. She has taught me so much about myself in the years we have known each other, without which I would never have thought myself capable of The Walk or many other worthwhile things, for that matter.

As it turns out, with Kelly's initial help, I got stronger by the day and fell totally in love with the thrill of fighting wildfires. I slowly began to replace winged eyeliner and layers of foundation with sweat and dirt. Self-consciousness gave way to gritty determination. I was hooked and never looked back at dispatch.

Maybe it was that transformation that encouraged me to do The Walk. It seems like the things I have no business doing are the exact things that change my life forever.

The four of us posed for a photo sleepily behind the Mt. Whitney Trail sign before hugging Mom and Dad goodbye. I eyed my mom a little warily because in all my thirty years on this planet I have only seen her tear up a couple of times—this was one of them, and I wasn't entirely sure why. As we walked away my dad shouted into the darkness, "God be with these hikers. Amen!" It gave me goosebumps, and still does.

Our group of four bobbing headlights took its first steps through the wooden structure signifying the start gate of Mt. Whitney around 3:15 a.m.

At exactly 3:25 a.m., I was hungry.

Josh was in the lead and setting a speedy pace, so I knew there was no stopping to take a snack break. My four years in fire had taught me an important lesson: keep something edible within arm's reach. On September 25, somewhere around 3:26 a.m., I was ripping open the top of a white powdered donut pack, scarfing them down as fast as I could. Step, scarf, step, scarf. It was not a good feeling, trying to suck in white, powdered air while hiking, but there's never any compromise when my stomach has a vote.

After maybe an hour of staring at nothing but my small headlamp beam on the toes of my shiny new shoes, I came running smack into the back of Kelly.

Well! My group had stopped to take a quick rest. I took this time to shed some layers (I was sweating like a stuffed pig) and munch a few more snacks from the enormous lunch my mom had made for me. It was so darned dark. And I was tired, sweaty, and perturbed as to what decisions I had made in life to get me here. Shawn stepped into the lead and I fell in behind him. That little sweetheart then set a pace that he knew was more my style, one where I could stuff things in my mouth and walk at the same time with minimal choking.

Onward and upward. I did notice one small-framed girl leapfrogging us, who I noted was wearing a tiny backpack and seemed to be alone. Alone! I could never have made this trek by myself, so I can't help but remember her. There were other random hikers too. I could hear them talking every now and then, and a few times I looked above me in the darkness and saw dozens of little lights snaking back and forth, making

8

me dizzy. A few hours later, we found ourselves at a creek crossing. The solo girl was stopped in front of us on a rock, trying to cross. When I saw her my first thought was, Why the heck isn't she moving? What a wimp, it is just a creek! But when I started to step into the creek, I realized why. The rocks were slicker than a politician, lingering just above the freezing, ice-chunked water. We all came to a slow stop, assessing the situation, when in a flash my big brother bounded by me to save the damsel in distress, no less. Except that this wasn't a movie, and the rocks were slippery, the creek was *so* cold and *very* wet. He slipped and had no choice but to splash in. Ever the gentleman, he stood proudly in that creek and held his hand out to the girl, then to me, then to Kelly. I always knew Josh was a sweet guy, but not put-your-feet-in-an-alpine-creek-at-5am-when-you-still-have-18-miles-to-go sweet. It was dark and cold, and we predicted it would only get colder and we'd hit snow drifts as we ascended, yet, there he was: wet shoes and grinning.

I was horrified. I had an extra pair of dry socks in my pack for such an occasion. Another useful thing working in fire had taught me is that if the worst thing is no snacks, the second worst is wet feet. I offered them to him, but he declined, and we kept caterpilling on up the mountain. Such a jolly fellow so early in the morning. I can't be entirely certain he's not adopted.

At 6:45 a.m., after about three and a half hours of navigating the heavy darkness, the sun began to bless us with its presence. By then, we had ascended above the tree line apparently, because as the light began to illuminate the world around us, it was not at all what I had been visualizing in my mind. Steep granite walls on both sides, granite boulders, granite peaks in the background, granite, granite, granite. If that doesn't sound magnificent to you, I get it. Before this particular moment in my life, it wouldn't have sounded that way to me either. But man, it was. More experienced adventurers might refer to it as "alpenglow," but I felt like I was on another planet; the yellow and pink hues splashing across the rock were otherworldly. Either that or I was just already so tired and hungry that everything seemed more vivid but seems to me my cohorts felt similar awe and wonder because we stopped to look around and snap a few pictures.

Kelly moved into the lead, and we started on. My naive brain was thinking I should be warmer now, since the sun was awake, but that

Granite, granite, everywhere.

couldn't have been more wrong. I kept snapping pictures on my phone as we went, still totally fascinated by this strange new landscape. I started to fall farther and farther behind Josh and Kelly, taking too many blurry pictures but excited nonetheless, Shawn staying right behind me. This was a developing theme not only on Mt. Whitney but for the entirety of The Walk. Shawn Milligan is one athletic guy, and I know for a fact he could have easily flown on by and made it to the top long before the rest of us, but if he was tempted to I never knew it. He stuck with me every single step, and trust me, some of those were very slow and painful steps. And that, my friends, is true love.

It was somewhere at this point Shawn turned to me, randomly, and said, "I wonder if there is going to be an old man at the top of this mountain, you know? Like, one who has all the answers to life! It just seems fitting that there would be."

"Wait. What?"

I burst out laughing/wheezing at this weird thought of his, but then, that is yet another one of my favorite things about the guy. He's, uh, unique.

We continued walking as Shawn pondered his profound statement, and I paid for my decision to take pictures; even after I put my gloves back on, my fingers ached to the bone with cold. Josh and Kelly were creating quite the gap ahead of me, so they stopped after a couple of switchbacks to wait for Shawn and me to catch up.

Ah, switchbacks. Mt. Whitney is famed for those bad boys, and this particular section had ninety-nine of them in a row.

Ninety-nine.

If I think about any one in particular, my right knee twinges. Kelly took off sometime around switchback number ten, and we wouldn't see her again until much later. It kind of reminded me of the cartoons, where smoke is coming up from the soles of the roadrunner's shoes as a flash of color zooms by. I was jealous of Kelly's energy. Josh, Shawn, and I kept weaving our way up the mountain, and this was the first time I noticed the effects of the altitude—we were somewhere in the 12,000-foot range so I guess it made sense. My breathing was getting raspy and I had one hell of a headache. As I looked at my super-fit older brother, I realized he was feeling it too. His face had lost all color and he was being really, un-brotherlike quiet. In case of such a scenario, we had brought along two small bottles of oxygen that I had found on Amazon, so I encouraged him to use them. I am not sure if they helped any, but he's got the heart of a lion, that man, so he kept putting one foot in front of the other, regardless.

Ever the pessimist, I had read up on altitude sickness prior to that day on Whitney. I knew that it was no joke, and that it doesn't matter whatsoever the physical fitness of the individual. Everyone reacts to high altitude differently, and one tip the pros give is to be sure to acclimate yourself a little bit before taking such huge leaps in elevation. We hadn't done that exactly, as we were unable to get a campsite at Whitney Portal the day before. We had camped at Lone Pine campground, which was a sweet little camp spot, but only sat at 6,000 feet. I watched Josh like a hawk after that, or at least I thought I did. I was feeling almost hungover and a bit wobbly myself.

One portion of the switchbacks included cables linking poles together to form a haphazard handrail. I was thankful for this as we found ourselves navigating snow and ice on our left, a sheer drop-off to our right. Going up didn't seem too overly sketchy, but I imagined that going down that sucker with my noodle legs would be truly terrifying.

One of my favorite parts of the Whitney hike, other than when it was over and I had a beer in my hand of course, sat at the top of those ninety-nine switchbacks: Trail Crest. This is the point in the hike where you start around the backside of the massive granite peaks we'd been staring at for the last three or so hours. At a little over 8 miles from our starting point, Trail Crest sits at 13,700 feet above sea level.

The view from Trail Crest took whatever breath I had left away. We stopped to take it all in and Shawn got this panorama:

The view from Trail Crest.

I was, and still am, fascinated with this view. It is like nothing I have ever seen. Somewhat loopy and increasingly off-kilter we trekked on, uplifted by the beauty that surrounded us along with the possibility that we could absolutely plummet to our deaths.

I was giddy. I am telling you I ran the whole gamut of emotions that day several times over, and at this particular moment I was on the pendulum upswing. Not ten minutes later we rounded a corner and I came to a screeching halt, gasping probably a bit too dramatically.

"Oh my God, Shawn, it's *HIM!*"

Shawn came to a stop behind me and quickly started shushing me. But I wasn't easily subdued, pointing my finger and bouncing on the balls of my cushy new shoes. There in front of me, sitting cross-legged on a precarious-looking boulder, sat an old man with skin the color of tanned leather, a long white beard, and a pleasant smile on his wise, weathered face.

I was laughing somewhat maniacally. My God, Shawn had been right. There was an old man at the top of the mountain with all of life's answers. I wanted to drop my pack and hug him.

I think Shawn had it more together than I did, and he was quickly trying to nudge me and talk over my inappropriate laughter. I am not that crass in normal life, but nothing is normal at 13,700 feet. We chatted for a few minutes with him, or Shawn did; I didn't catch much of their conversation because I was too busy staring, grinning, bouncing. At some point they wrapped up their pleasantries and we meandered off. We passed several other people on the mountain that day, but none had the effect on me that that sweet man had.

More than one fellow hiker had, however, noticed the little yellow tags that were swinging happily to and fro on the outside of our packs. These were the day passes we were required to hang in a noticeable spot, should we be checked by a ranger, or an alien, or a marmot, or whatever. The very unpleasant guy at the Lone Pine Visitor's Center was specific in his instructions when we picked up our passes. He also had zero sense of humor, unfortunately.

Getting the passes in the first place wasn't easy, as nothing on this trek would prove to be. My original plan was to recreate my dad's journey as closely as possible, which would mean we would get an overnight pass and sleep at Trail Camp (located at the base of ninety-nine switchbacks) before summiting Mt. Whitney and officially starting our walk from the highest to the lowest point. It was also my goal to do this hike at the same age he did, thirty years old. I cooked up this hair-brained idea about a year and a half prior, so I figured cutting through the appropriate red tape would be no big thing. I was sufficiently wrong about that, too. In order to get the much sought-after overnight passes, you had to enter a lottery. *Okie dokie.*

I mulled this information over for a few days, reading everything I could on what to do next. I submitted my entry on the very first day the lottery opened, February 1, 2017. My plan was to have each one of the Sandwalkers enter too, increasing my odds by—I don't know—like 25 percent? Math has never been my strong suit. Too bad my cleverness was thwarted when I realized you were required to list the names of each person in your party, after which they would be prohibited from submitting their own entry. There was a fee, too. I filled out the form, entered my debit card information, held my breath, and clicked "submit."

Just exactly like every lottery I have ever played, I didn't win. On March 24, I received an email saying, "We are sorry to inform you that your application to Mt Whitney Lottery 2017 was not successful." I was *crushed*. I called the number I found online, and a chipper woman encouraged me to wait until May 1, when they would release all the permits that hadn't been claimed, effectively giving me a second chance at this big dream of mine.

So I waited. On May 1, a Monday, I hopped online first thing and... nothing. I watched and I checked and I waited. By the time night fell, I knew I wasn't getting an overnight pass to Mt. Whitney. I distinctly remember crying and being consoled by my mom, via cell phone, and Shawn, via a dry shoulder. This wasn't the year I would make my big adventure to honor my daddy.

Maybe next year, they told me.

It took a few days, but eventually I had to resign myself to this fate, maybe next year this dream would become a reality. *Sandwalkers, 2018, here I come!* That thought gave me a dry and bitter taste in my mouth, but I tried to put it behind me and move on.

Fast-forward a bit: I was about to start my fourth fire season with the Forest Service and was down soaking in the sunshine of southern California with my parents before I got too busy to see them. I got to commiserating/drinking with my dad and he mentioned that, hey, maybe you could get a day pass up Mt. Whitney—you know, keep the dream alive. I chewed on that for a few minutes. I had never considered the day pass because it wasn't what Dad did, but the more we talked, the more enticing it got. It could have been the beers too. Who knows?

Anyway, what Dad had been remembering was his hike from Trail Camp up to Whitney and then back down to the portal. It wasn't easy, obviously, but he was sure we could survive that route. It was around 16 miles. Painful, but doable. He even remembers having plenty of daylight left.

Okie dokie.

We cracked another beer, got online, and started searching. The problem was, due to work schedules, we only had a small window to be able to start The Walk. With three of us being in fire, we had to shoot for a time when the fire season was winding down, but too late in the year meant hitting snow on the mountain. The sweet spot was September 25, 2017, which was the same date I had entered in the overnight lottery but didn't win.

I am going to stop right here and say: if you don't believe in divine intervention, this is where you should probably just chuck this book into the fireplace and walk away, because you won't believe much of the rest of it anyway. There was exactly one date available for the day-hiking permit, September 25, and there were *exactly* four spots left. Well gee, I happen to know three other people as nuts as I am, so I booked it. It cost me somewhere around $70 to get the permits for all of us. Just one text to Harper and a "Let's do this!" reply, and it was done.

It's funny, what Dad failed to realize was that they made camp six and a half miles above the starting point. This allowed them to reach the top of Whitney and return back to the trailhead in full light the following day. Another caveat was that he had done the hike in June of '74, so he had much more daylight than we would have in September. Add all this up and I was looking at a 22-mile hike on the first day of a 131-mile trek, in which I had to make it to the top and back with all my body parts intact so that I could continue on the rest of my journey.

Sweet.

This is how us SSIIs (Sandwalkers: Second Edition) came to be toting the cute little yellow tags on the zippers of our packs. I didn't think anything of it, until several hikers we met on the trail mentioned them. "Day hikers!" some whispered.

"Are you really doing this in one day?? What time did you leave!?"

Shawn got a big kick out of this for some reason: "Day hikers" he would hiss at me and swell his chest up like Superman. There was some sort of demented pride going on here, some of which I took part in. At the same time, I couldn't help but think of how dumb and unlucky we were to not have won the overnight pass and to try instead this risky yellow-tag thing.

"Congrats on the lottery," I'd mutter back.

At some point or another, we found Kelly tucked away on a rock, admiring the view and waiting for us slow pokes, I presumed. We sat down to join her while I inhaled an entire Costco chocolate chip muffin. Josh was still pale and too quiet, so we kept forcing oxygen on him. I still had my ridiculous headache, so I also partook in the oxygen. Shawn seemed totally unaffected by it all, except that when I looked over at him laughing and babbling away, I noticed something off about his face.

I knew that face like it was my own, had spent three years to the day studying it, so I could tell something wasn't quite right. It was his lips, which were a cobalt shade of blue, so I forced the oxygen bottle on him too, muffin crumbs and all.

We stood and Josh stowed his pack behind a rock so that he wouldn't have to haul it the rest of the way to the top. I had planned on stowing mine too, but Shawn wouldn't even consider leaving his, so I decided against it. Plus, there were a lot of snacks in there. Unfortunately, Josh had the oxygen in his pack, so we left that behind, reminiscent of exactly what my dad had done forty-three years ago.

What caused us to leave the oxygen behind? Well, lack of oxygen of course.

This space in my memory is so strange. I know we had a couple more miles before reaching the summit, but they are just sort of granite-colored blurs in my mind. I guess this is what altitude does to you, makes you feel drunk, but not in the fun sort of way. I came to when we were on the home stretch, well, of the up part anyway. I remember being in the back of the pack again, Shawn behind me, when my cohorts stopped and pushed me suddenly to the front.

"This was your idea, lead us on in, With!"

Well, that sweet gesture got me all sorts of emotional, and tears streamed down my face as we summited Mt. Whitney around 11 a.m., a mere 8 hours after starting our adventure.

High fives. Blur.

Pretty view. More blur.

Taking pictures. Blurrrrr.

It is so funny, during all of this time Shawn was strangely absent. I took pictures with Josh and Kelly and marveled at my surroundings, trying to wrap my head around what we had just accomplished. Shawn was bent over his pack, rummaging through it for what he claimed was a tissue so that he could blow his nose. OK.

Blur.

He finally stood up and joined us in a group photo. Someone had randomly procured a sign that read "Mt. Whitney, 14,508 feet," which was pretty neat, but I have no idea where it came from. We posed, triumphant.

Shawn and I then posed together for what I thought was a photo

The smiles on our faces indicate that we forgot . . . this is where "The Walk" starts.

on top of the highest mountain in the contiguous United States. After I thought we had taken it, he turned to me and we kissed and hugged, during which he wished me a Happy Anniversary. This is also a blur, so I am darn lucky that Josh was indeed videotaping, not taking a photo like I was led to believe. In the next instant, Shawn was mumbling something like, "I know we are going to have our highs and our lows, we just have to make our highs better than our lows."

Say what?

You could have stuck Newton's law of gravitation equation in front of me and I wouldn't have been more confused. Every girl knows a diamond when she sees one though, and all of a sudden the man of my dreams was holding something shiny up at me and asking me to marry him. I have never burst into tears on cue before and I didn't really know if that was a real-life thing, but I can say now with certainty that it is. And I did. I wasn't even able to form the one syllable word "yes." I just furiously nodded my head up and down, but I guess he got the point.

There were other people on the top of Mt. Whitney at that wonderful moment in the history of my life, so once I calmed down I noticed how

A whole lot of love at 14,508 feet.

awkwardly quiet it was. I untucked my head from Shawn's shoulder and took a peek. Everyone was staring at us. Shawn, ever the entertainer, did a big fist pump in the air and hollered, "She said yes!" and people clapped. I mean, they clapped. Really. Girls, if you are reading this, wait for your fairytale. I swear it is out there and it is worth the wait.

THROWING A SUPPORT PARTY

—Jim—

We had no sooner set up camp the afternoon before The Walk when Josh stood and said, "Let's hike up a ways and see where the Whitney Portal trail comes into the campground." I could see where that would be a good thing to know, seeing as how the Sandwalkers Second Edition would be coming in that way, eventually, if all went well. That trail wasn't there when we made the original trek back in 1974—we'd walked the perilously narrow highway down from Whitney Portal—so I wasn't able to advise them on the trail's location or suitability.

Shawn begged off saying he had some more stuff to get ready, but I soon found he just wanted to be rid of them for the moment. As soon as everybody was out of earshot, Val included, he sat down across from me and fessed up: "I asked Josh to get them away because I wanted to talk to you," he said, gaining my attention, which at times wasn't all that easy. But I was certainly the expert to come to if you had questions about this trip, which he apparently did, so I was all ears. Without missing a beat, however, he went completely off my neatly-laid-out rails: "I love your daughter very much, and I'd like to ask for her hand in marriage."

Well.

I picked my jaw up off the picnic table, hoping to proceed coherently from there, but it was not to be.

Well.

I was much older than Shawn, but I had no idea suitors still did that, if they're still called suitors. Ask for hands in marriage, I mean.

Well, um... I couldn't seem to speak and my eyes teared up.

Well.

I was very pleased, but completely flummoxed and unable to utter anything at all, so I balled up my fist and offered a bump, which he happily

19

returned. I'm not sure exactly what I finally said, but I think it was something on the order of, "That would just tickle me plumb to death, Shawn."

If not for the fist bump the whole thing would have seemed even more old-timey than it was. We sealed the deal with a couple bottles of India Pale Ale, which was, appropriately, the modern version of an age-old British colonial invention.

Shawn told me he intended to propose to Withanee when they reached the summit of Mt. Whitney tomorrow, so he swore me to secrecy for the time being. Not a problem, I assured him, as this information was going to take a while to trickle down.

If I were to make this into a movie, what we'd leap to here is: [*Camera backs away and fade-out, followed by fade-in to campground the following sunshiny morning.*] One has to wonder why I'm not in Hollywood, but the Support Party Narrative really begins here, *sans* camera—you'll just have to use your old-timey imagination.

In the early morning sunshine Mt. Whitney loomed beyond Lone Pine Campground like a great unwelcome guest; forty-three years ago I'd spent the coldest, most miserable night of my life up there, followed closely by the coldest, most miserable day of my life. My daughter, along with her fiancé-to-be, my stepson, and her coworker were at this very moment climbing up there somewhere, presumably cold and miserable and no doubt wishing they hadn't been so anxious to embark on this trip.

"This trip" was to be a reincarnation of my seven-day 1974 walk from the highest point in the contiguous forty-eight states to the lowest point in the Western hemisphere, which had started in misery, proceeded in misery, and ended in misery. Only in utmost hindsight did it become somewhat bearable, which apparently was the part that sank into my daughter's pliable mind as she grew up.

My bad.

At any rate, that was how I ended up in this campground with my wife, Val, the two of us providing support for the hikers. We were in a 25-foot Minnie Winnie motor home that we'd rented for the week, backed tightly into space 4 alongside a wooden picnic bench and, appropriately, a Lone Pine. Snugged against the front bumper was my '93 Toyota 4Runner and across the access road, in Space 3, was Kelly Harper's pickup alongside Josh's Subaru. Before we'd turned in last night, we also erected three tents around a nearby fire ring (Kelly slept in her pickup), so we had a monopoly on the immediate neighborhood, which was a good thing; at two o'clock *in the morning* we'd fired up a gasoline generator in order to make coffee for our hiker/victims. I'm sure the racket woke everybody in the campground, but at least we were isolated enough that they didn't have to breathe the exhaust fumes.

And I could pencil another "first" into my ever-expanding résumé; never before, in over seven decades, had I ever set an alarm for 1:50 a.m., praise God. The hikers were up and about and cheerfully ready to go before I even had my eyes properly opened, but that's how it is with the young. No wonder there are species on this planet that eat 'em. By the time I was actually awake and functioning I was in the driver's seat of the 4Runner with Val beside me, the hiker's backpacks and equipment taking up the rear seats and cargo space, while the hikers themselves were just pulling out in Josh's Subaru, headed for the trailhead at Whitney Portal.

We followed as swiftly as my twenty-four-year-old 4-cylinder engine could pull us up the steep incline, which wasn't very swift at all. By the time we reached the trailhead parking lot our hikers were milling about in the crisp darkness with a lot more exuberance than I recalled in the original Sandwalkers. They unloaded their equipment, kitted up and— interrupted by a lot of hugging and handshaking—turned and began the first leg of their trip. In the inky morning darkness all we could see as they started out was their headlamps bouncing along up the trail, resembling Snow White's dwarves headed for the mine. I was going to belt out, "Hi-ho hi-ho, it's off to work we go," but what came out was something on the order of: "Lord, watch over these hikers today!" You could tell it was louder than most prayers because it was answered with a whole slew of "AMENS" suggesting there was more anxiety on the Mt. Whitney trail that morning than was brought by our four Sandwalkers.

As soon as their lights bobbed away into darkness, Val and I, being used to southern Nevada, fairly jumped back into the 4Runner and turned on the heater. We looped past the lodge and back down the road, and I told Val about the coming engagement of our daughter. She started crying a little before or maybe a little after I did, but in spite of our weepy trip back to the Mini Winnie, neither Val nor I had a bit of trouble dropping instantly into deep sleep.

When we awoke the sun was fully up, and we greeted it with coffee at the picnic table, which offered a good long-distance view of Mt. Whitney.

It didn't look very promising as the wispy clouds above the summit were shredding, indicative of the awful wind we encountered those many years ago. And if it was cold and windy where Val and I sat way down here at the campground, which it was, I feared a howling arctic gale way up there was slapping the bejesus out of the Second Edition, just as it had us original morons. But if that were so there wasn't anything Val and I could do about it, so we retired to the nearest tent where we could still see the mountain but be out of the wind. And we fell asleep again. As an aside, our hikers experienced no wind at all on Mt. Whitney. How that could possibly be, in spite of all the indications to the contrary, is beyond me. I would later see Withanee's video, and the rarefied air up there was as still as a midsummer morning. That just does not happen.

We woke up when Val got stung by a bee, which just does not happen around here either. Well, OK; it happened to me once on that miserable mountain forty-three years ago. We were at Outpost Camp at 10,000 feet just below timberline when we stopped for a downhill break along with an uninvited, cranky, possibly oxygen-starved bumblebee. It was pert' near the last misery inflicted upon myself by Mister Mt. Whitney, the *very* last being swollen knees from the steep, rapid descent I insisted upon. You can only take so much from a stupid mountain, after all, and I just couldn't wait to get off that cold granite and out into the welcoming friendly desert. (What should come to mind here is, "Be careful what you pray for.")

Be that as it may, Val's bee sting wasn't near as painful as mine was. I could tell because I didn't hear any howling like I did last time. As far as I could see at the time, Val's bee sting was the first of the parallels connecting the "original" walk with the current attempt. Unfortunately, it was not to be the last, nor, as I found out later from the folks now up on the mountain, was it in actuality the first. The first would be leaving the oxygen cylinders, intended for use on the summit, somewhere below in carefully stashed backpacks.

But the sting did get us up and going (original walk connection #2), which more or less set the routine we'd be using for the remainder of The Walk; daily excursions to the nearest store, gas station, and/or RV station to replenish and refresh our supplies. Even though I had a pretty good idea of what was going to be required for our walkers to pull this off there were a lot of if's, maybe's, and what-now's that, even if anticipated somewhat, needed to be taken care of on a daily basis. Today we'd drive the

4Runner into Lone Pine for provisions, leaving the Minnie Winnie at the campsite, an option we hoped to repeat as much as possible. In keeping with their names, motor *homes* are best left by themselves somewhere—they're not conducive to shopping and are particularly offended by traffic, narrow streets, and parallel or even angled parking.

We drove the 6 miles into Lone Pine, although it was hard to turn our backs to the mountain. It was almost as if we were playing hooky, abandoning our charges so we could take on the guise of responsible adults.

The small town of Lone Pine has a surprisingly large and well-stocked Mom and Pop grocery store where we found everything we needed, and as a bonus Val enthralled the two young checkout ladies with the tale of our daughter's pending engagement on the summit of Mt. Whitney. I'd been around quite a while, and girl talk had heretofore bored me to tears, but not this time. This time the tears came from somewhere else. I was glad to get out of there and back into my manly 4Runner where I could hang my arm out the window and shift gears.

We'd only gone a couple of blocks when Val's cellphone rang. If it was Withanee it would be around the time she would be getting engaged, but cellphone coverage being what it was, a call from her would be highly unlikely, perhaps impossible.

However, it *was* Withanee, improbably calling from the summit of Mt. Whitney. She was actually sending us a live video to Val's phone. I somehow pulled off the road without causing any obvious fatalities, and there she was on the small screen. She was excited but breathless. I expected that at 14,000+ feet, but I didn't expect her hair to be lying calmly across her forehead as if all were windless and serene up there, which she then confirmed. The wind was still blowing in Lone Pine, and a quick glance at the mountaintops proved the cloud wisps were still shredding. How odd. Odder still was the fact that she was able to call out on her phone—apparently nobody else was able to, and she was unable to repeat it a few minutes later. There was a time when I thought things like these just happened, coincidental-like. However, as my daughter mentioned in the first chapter, if you don't believe in divine intervention you're going to have to reconsider if you read much further.

In the video we got to glimpse the dazzling engagement ring on her hand and I also had to admit to everybody that Shawn had already cleared the proposal with me, so I guess I was guilty of withholding important stuff from my child. Again. Val had already given me my withholding scolding this morning, so everything was good now, right?

We headed back to camp, realizing that we'd been thrown for a loop on this one, but content that it was a pleasant loop and worth every one of Shawn's and my misdeeds.

Mostly Shawn's, of course.

SWITCHBACK IS A FOUR-LETTER WORD

— Withanee —

Everything after the proposal was a flurry. Hugs and tears from my fellow Sandwalkers reminded me that I absolutely had to call my parents with the news. Here again, divine intervention. I hadn't had cell service the entire way up Mt. Whitney, not one single bar, and I didn't have any when we were taking our photos before the proposal. But, all of a sudden when I needed it most, I had full bars on my phone to be able to FaceTime Mom and Dad who sat somewhere far in the valley below.

Looking back, I wish we would have somehow recorded this conversation. I remember showing them my sparkling ring, and I remember Dad not fully believing we were on top of Mt. Whitney because my hair wasn't blowing, nor was I bundled up shivering. Actually, after I had frozen my fingers off before the switchbacks, the weather totally flipped and we began shedding layers. It was a gorgeous, perfect, and well, divine day. After we hung up, I tried sending a couple of texts out to my aunts and best friend, though I think only one went through before the service completely disappeared again. Hmm.

I got up off of the rock I had been sitting on and walked over to my group, who were huddled up together, smiling. My big brother, who hadn't brought his pack and had forgotten the oxygen, had somehow managed to remember a flask of Sarsaparilla. We each took a pull in cheers to our engagement and this being the official start of The Walk.

We turned to go, and I stumbled over to the old weather station building in which my dad had hid from the bitter wind forty-three years ago. There was a ledger to sign, and Josh had already signed "Sandwalkers V2," but I had to shakily add something. It read, "Engaged on top of Mt. Whitney, Shawn & Withanee." Wow.

In my fuzzy, altitude-ridden brain I knew I wasn't just about to embark on the adventure of a lifetime in The Walk but also in my life's adventure with Shawn. The meaning wasn't lost on me, and I appreciated that quick moment of clarity to savor for the next couple of miles.

Down we went, into the wild blue yonder. The high from the top of Mt. Whitney carried me a couple of miles when the harsh reality of my physical condition started to slap me in the face. I have to say, when I started my career in fire I had never run more than a mile. I had never hiked carrying a heavy pack. I wasn't tough. I wasn't in shape, so I thought I knew the full definition of the word "sore" from having dealt with it in spades back then while training for my first fire season. Wrong again. Aches and pains were starting to pop up like sucker punches as we wound our way back down toward Trail Crest.

One fun distraction though was whooping and encouraging the hikers that were on their way up, looking as miserable and exhausted as we had been only a few hours ago. We talked to some, high-fived others, even met a little boy who was making the climb with his dad. It was a neat camaraderie that everyone shared: all of us on a sketchy trail 14,000 feet in the air, just one loose rock away from plummeting to our deaths in an attempt of doing something memorable. Here is an interesting statistic: only one-third of the hikers who give it a go even summit Mt. Whitney. Looking at it now, it feels pretty good to be a part of that club.

At the time though, it didn't. Going down was so much harder than going up, and going up was *hard*. The only thing that got easier was the breathing. I felt like I was starting to sober up from the lack of oxygen as we began zigzagging down those stupid switchbacks. With that came the realization of what had actually happened up there. Holy cow! I was *engaged!* It was like slowly waking up from a dream. The only way to remind myself I hadn't totally imagined the whole thing was that sparkle beaming up at me from my left hand and my grinning new fiancé. Wow. If this is what drugs feel like, I suppose I can understand why people get addicted.

We all unanimously decided that "switchback" is a four-letter word, and when we finally got to the bottom of the 99, we stopped for a lunch break. Kelly plopped down and yanked off her shoes, laying her head on her pack for what looked to be one glorious five-minute stint.

Five minutes was about it though. Josh was perking up significantly, and his energy had returned in full force in the thin, 12,000-foot air. He was hopping up and sliding into his pack before I had even finished chewing my sandwich.

"We better get goin'!" he grinned.

We all stared warily up at him.

"But...haven't even got to...tato chips," I grunted back, mouth full and body too exhausted for politeness.

He said nothing but kept grinning at me. Ugh.

The three of us slowly got to our feet, and with Josh in the lead we started in on the 6 miles we had left for the day. At some point in the next few minutes, I felt a pain coming on that I had never felt before in my right knee. It didn't make a popping sound or anything obvious like that, but developed more like a toothache does—throbbing, painful, annoying. It didn't take long to develop into a pitiful limp. All I can say about that is, *thank God for trekking poles*. What started out as a balance mechanism going up the mountain turned into crutches that were supporting most of my weight going down. I wouldn't have made it without them.

I wouldn't have made it without my fellow hikers, either. The further down we went, the more miserable my knee became, the rest of my body following suit. Those guys kept me laughing, and we couldn't stop fantasizing about the fried chicken my mom had promised to cook for us that night. Kelly, the oddest vegetarian you will ever meet, has a soft spot for chicken, so it sort of became a cadence chant: fried chicken, fried chicken, fried chicken.

We didn't see too many people after that, but I do remember two older gentlemen coming quickly down the trail behind us. I actually heard them trampling up before I even saw them. That made me feel pretty bad about myself, having resorted to a hunched over limping ball of misery by then. I stepped aside to watch these white-haired fellows fly by me.

And fly, they did. The leader whipped his legs out in front of his body a little too rambunctiously, losing control and sprawling to the ground like a runner stealing base. Shawn saw it coming and tried to put his hand out to catch him, to no avail, and he came sliding to a stop in a cloud of dust right in front of our feet. I froze, shocked. Shawn tried to reach down to help him up, but apparently his old man pride wasn't about to let that happen. He jumped up with more dexterity than I could ever have mustered at that point and went on his way. I swear, if I had blinked, I'd have missed the whole thing.

Fried chicken. Fried chicken. Fried chicken.

We kept thinking we were closer to the bottom than we were. Having come up this leg of the journey in the pitch darkness of 3 a.m., we had no landmarks with which to compare. Although the scenery was beautiful now that we could see it, I stopped caring after a while and was solely focused on shuffling one foot in front of the other. Josh had a small bar of service every now and then, so when he could, he would text Mom to tell her when we figured we would be arriving.

We figured wrong. It could have been my pained pace, but it took much longer than we expected. The sun had set and it was just getting dark by the time we finally spotted the end of the trail, where our support party awaited us with all the excitement of what felt like a war hero's homecoming parade.

We loaded back up in the two vehicles and drove the windy road back down to our campsite. That night, we regaled our support party with stories, ate the best-fried chicken I've ever had, drank our well-deserved beers, and sort of just basked in the glory of it all. I will never forget Mom and Dad's faces as they watched the video of Shawn's proposal. I am so, so glad they were there to celebrate with us.

Well, day one down.

FRIED CHICKEN AND... FRIED *ENGINE?*

—Jim—

When we got back to our campsite we no sooner had unloaded when Val started organizing the evening meal. She had decided, in her orderly little mind, that she'd whip up a fried chicken dinner complete with mashed potatoes, gravy, corn, and biscuits for six people, at least four of whom would be borderline ravenous.

I spent a couple of months in a small motor home, and I once owned a restaurant, so I was fully aware that with the space and resources available up here at the Lone Pine Campground there was just no way to fix a meal like she had in mind for that many people. But would she listen? No. She gave me a bottle of India Pale Ale and told me to go sit at the picnic table and keep an eye on Mt. Whitney. Now I'm not an idiot, and I knew she just wanted to get me out of the way; however, watching that contrary mountain also seemed prudent, especially when you're armed with an IPA. So I dutifully went. Poor thing though, at best I knew she was just postponing my lilting refrain of "I told you so."

Having known Val for thirty-seven years, I suppose I should have been unsurprised and grateful for the pitifully few hours I'd have before I ate those words, along with fried chicken, mashed potatoes, gravy, corn, and biscuits.

Before that could come to pass though we'd have to return to Whitney Portal and bring back our hikers, or more accurately, their packs. We'd convoyed them up this morning and now we'd have to convoy them back, then turn around and take the hikers back up in the morning; the Second Edition would have to start tomorrow's walk where they left off today, naturally, and since the few spaces at Whitney Portal Campground were assigned on a first-come-first-served basis we had elected not to depend on the availability of vacant campsites up there. By reserving spaces a few miles away at Lone Pine Campground well in advance, we were assured of a place to sleep even if it required a lot of shuttling back and forth.

So shuttle we did, this time in the early evening, hoping to get some pictures of our charges striding triumphantly down the trail into Whitney Portal. We got the pictures all right, but the trek down took longer than expected and the Second Edition Sandwalkers didn't look particularly triumphant. Truth to tell, they looked pretty ragged. I suppose that was to be expected as they made the entire climb from trailhead to summit and back in a single day. The original Sandwalkers spent one night at the 12,000-foot-high Trail Camp before summiting and returning the following day, mainly because trail permits were easy to come by in those days. In today's world, however, it's done by a drawing much like the lottery, with about the same odds of winning. It nearly broke Withanee's heart when she lost out on that overnight permit.

She could still retry for a one-day trip permit for the summit, but only an idiot would suggest she apply for something that severe.

Well it wouldn't take a *total* idiot, of course; it's entirely possible for a well-meaning Whitney veteran to kind of misremember camping overnight at Trail Camp thereby shortening the climbing day by *lots*. I would certainly give a guy like that the benefit of a doubt, as might most Christians this side of the Pearly Gates, don't you think? And there was also an upside; The Walk itself would thus be shortened by one full day. Not a big thing at the moment of course, but a big-one-to-be by the end of the week. Probably.

After some tentative pain-avoidance hugging, a lot of high-fives and a special welcome to the newly engaged couple, the Second Edition loaded their gear into the 4Runner and followed us down in Josh's Subaru, which he'd left in the trailhead parking lot a couple of years ago this morning.

It was almost dark so I turned on the headlights, not wanting to tempt fate on this winding downgrade. I didn't like it forty-three years ago and nothing had changed my mind on this trip. Long before I met up with Whitney Portal Road, Humphrey Bogart had fishtailed wildly coming up these curves on the silver screen in 1941's *High Sierra,* and Lucille Ball and Desi Arnaz nearly had heart failure trying to negotiate this very road in 1953's *The Long, Long Trailer.* I may be the only person in the world who ever had a cheerful micro-moment up here in 1974 when Ken Oberg came down with a toe blister near the rock-walled hairpin curve. We still had a long walk ahead of us to get to Badwater, but I was terribly happy that someone besides me was going to be wearing moleskin. On Whitney Portal Road any joy at all that bubbles to the surface is worthy of a marble monument, but it never lasts long enough to carve one.

It didn't this time either. My 4Runner felt funny when I downshifted to get more braking action. It didn't slow down like it ought to or like it did before. It crossed my mind that our Whitney hikers had brought most of the summit down in their packs as souvenirs, but that was every bit as ridiculous as it sounded. So there was no extra weight pushing us along, as happened with *The Long, Long Trailer,* and there was no reason to be paranoid the way Bogart was, with good reason, in *High Sierra,* but something wasn't right. In spite of being in third gear, at times even dropping down into second, I wasn't getting any engine braking at all, and I had to ride the foot brake hard all the way down to the campground turnoff.

Josh's headlights were right behind us when we turned and he, along with the rest of the gang in the car with him, witnessed an explosion of smoke and oil from the 4Runners' tailpipe. He followed me in, trying to get my attention by flicking his headlights but I didn't notice. What I did notice was that the 4Runner seemed to be running funny; it lacked power going up the slight slope to the entrance, and as we started downhill into the campground I now had to step on the gas to maintain speed. What was *that* all about? Puzzled, I backed into our space, just barely, turned off the lights and switched off the engine. It clunked one time, like an oversized exclamation point at the end of a sentence.

I wasn't feeling content right about then, and even less so after I was told about the smoke explosion at the turnoff. I instinctively started to pop the hood but it was cold and dark and there was fried chicken waiting, so I hesitated just long enough to change my mind. We unloaded the cargo and, in a rare fit of wisdom, decided to discuss the 4Runner situation after dinner.

And man was that a great dinner. For me it was made even better by Val graciously declining to serve me a well-deserved side of crow, bless her heart. After the meal everything looked a lot better, but even at that it was still pretty bleak; if we'd just lost the ranging ability of the 4Runner we were in trouble. There was no way the motor home would go off-road when we needed to. Our original plan was to leave Josh's Subaru in Lone Pine and leapfrog the Minnie Winnie and the 4Runner as we went, then ferry the walkers back in the motor home after it was all over. Originally Kelly was going to leave her pickup in Lone Pine also, but she was unable to get the extra time off work and would be going home tomorrow.

So having no plan B, we had to come up with something other than India Pale Ale. It seemed sensible to plan for something that wouldn't require the use of the 4Runner, which could conceivably end up hanging off the end of a tow truck tomorrow. Chicken might not be the only thing that was fried this day.

Rather than cancel The Walk, Josh offered the use of his brand-new Subaru SUV. It was, after all, a full-time all-wheel-drive but it was low-slung and, worse, it was brand new. For Pete's sake, it was so modern it didn't even have an ignition key, not to mention the Star Trek dashboard it *did* have. New cars have always made me nervous, but I lump new twenty-first-century cars in the same bin with smart phones and Wi-Fi and iPads; they have no business bringing their electron-laden faces into my happy places.

However, if it meant the difference between canceling The Walk or carrying on, I supposed I could try to live with it for a week. And besides Val would be driving it, for the most part, while I shuttled the Minnie Winnie. Technology holds no terrors for anyone who can prepare a banquet in a 25-foot motor home.

Although it's not accepted as a solution to problems of any sort these days, before turning in we cast our cares in general, and my cares about the 4Runner in particular, upon the Lord. After all, He'd certainly given windless aid and comfort to our hikers up on the mountain today.

EVERYTHING HURTS

— *Withanee* —

We said our goodnights and all retired to our respective beds. I thought this would be the best part, having a full belly and one big accomplishment under my belt; I'd drift off into the hardest sleep I'd ever had. Right? Instead, as soon as I lay down in my sleeping bag, my entire body started *screaming* at me. Every single thing hurt, and not in an *I am uncomfortable and need to change positions* kind of way. I have never felt pain like that before The Walk, in which I felt it every single day. I tried to roll onto my side but couldn't manage to do it. Grunting, groaning, and squeezing back tears and profanity, I sat up and shook my head. This definitely wasn't going to work. Back to the Minnie Winnie I went, where I dug through our box of supplies and came up with a Costco sized bottle of Advil. I don't ever recall bringing that bottle back home after The Walk. I am inclined to believe it may have been empty by the end of the thing. I wonder how my liver is doing.

It took a while for the Advil to kick in, so I kind of just sat in my tent, thinking about the day. I never did figure out why I woke up wet that first morning. It hadn't rained, no one else was wet, and my tent windows were securely zippered. Huh. Night sweats, I suppose, condensed on the inside of my tent. I finally drifted off into a fitful, aching sleep, my last thought wondering what the heck I was doing out here.

The next morning dawned, and I sat up like the Crypt Keeper rising from his tomb. *Owwww.* Getting dressed was an Olympic sport, and I felt like I deserved a medal by the time I had stumbled out of my tent, somewhat upright.

I suspiciously eyed my cohorts. They were jolly, sipping coffee, and chatting like nothing had happened the day before. They even looked *limber,* moving about our campsite and gearing up for the day. No one else seemed to be hurting like I was, another theme that became painstakingly consistent for the next several days.

A couple more Advil down the hatch.

It was unfortunate, but in the last few weeks leading up to The Walk, Kelly couldn't secure all the time off she needed to come with us. She had been one of the first people to sign up to do this with me, so I can't say I wasn't disappointed that she wouldn't be carrying on, and I know she was disappointed too. That morning, she couldn't quite tear herself away, so she decided to walk the first 4 miles from Whitney Portal to our camp spot and enjoy breakfast with our little group before heading home.

Josh and Shawn had come up with an alternative route for that morning than what I had initially planned. The Original Sandwalkers, Dad and party, had followed the snaking Whitney Portal Road, which offered gorgeous views but little to no shoulder to walk/limp along. They went this way because at the time there was no other choice. Today though, there is a lovely trail that takes more of a direct route through the forest, then down along a ridgeline before dropping neatly into Lone Pine campground. Dad drove us back up to the Portal to begin the day's stretch and got this picture:

For me, collapse seems imminent.

We all held up two fingers to signify "day two" of however many it took to walk from the highest point (Mt. Whitney, check!) to the lowest point

(Badwater, Death Valley) in the contiguous United States. You may be able to tell by the photo; the moment I took my weight off the poles to hold up two fingers, my legs buckled beneath me. What an accurate portrayal of how I was feeling on the fine morning of day two.

There really is something to be said for having navigators, and those guys did great. I wasn't much of a leader in that respect, mainly because I was too focused on taking each step to care much about which way we were going. I also have a horrid sense of direction, a trait my mom and I share, so I was happy to hand off that little responsibility to the boys. The new route they came up with was pretty darn pleasant. The scenery was enjoyable, the temperature was warm, intermixed with a cool morning breeze; and our spirits were high. If it wasn't for my body's full-on war against me, I dare say I even enjoyed those miles.

We came strolling into the campground, following our noses to the wafting smell of scrambled eggs and sausage whipped up by the loving hands of my momma.

I am somewhat of a physical carbon copy of my mom, who stands at 5'2", though as a kid I thought she was 6 feet tall. You didn't mess with her; she had raised two boys before me, and she could always beat them at a foot race or wrestle them to the ground when the need arose, regardless of how big and strong they got.

A beautiful combination of grit and grace, my mom is truly unlike any other. When I was just a few years old, she was diagnosed with a brain tumor. There was only one surgeon in the country that would even attempt to remove it, and he gave her very little odds of survival. At the time, the medical community was going through a controversial phase of not using pain killers on patients. My mom was in a Pittsburgh hospital for a month undergoing several surgeries to remove the tumor, and they gave her small amounts of *Tylenol* for the pain. That is just the tip of the iceberg when it comes to how tough this woman is. There is nothing she can't do, and my dad and I learned long ago not to try to tell her otherwise.

That trait is probably one of the reasons she is so much fun. She is always game for any adventure, and in her world everything is possible. You will find her wearing high heels and pressed dresses at church or her job as a schoolteacher, or in ripped jeans and a faded tee digging and hauling dirt at their mine, cutting something with her chainsaw, or knee deep in some other project she has set her mind to. There is no in between.

Growing up is funny, isn't it? As a teenager, I know I drove her nuts. Like most mothers and daughters, we butted heads like big horned sheep. Eventually, that stubbornness fades away and there comes a time when kids realize what incredible people their parents are. Or at least I did. I call her every single day and get offended if she doesn't answer to hear about my day. I simply adore her.

So really, it was no surprise that she had a huge meal ready and waiting for us every time we came sauntering into camp. I can't cook for beans, even in a full-sized kitchen, and yet here she was, whipping up gourmet, home cooked meals for us on that teeny little motor home stove. What a gal.

After Mom's breakfast, we geared back up to head toward the town of Lone Pine. We said goodbye to Kelly and watched her little green Toyota pick-up sadly fade into the distance.

And then there were three.

I felt somewhat of a phantom limb pain without Kel and it took me some time to get used to her absence, though time is one thing I had plenty of, so I guess it worked out OK.

Some-odd, maybe 4 miles later we came to Lone Pine Creek. I took this opportunity to do exactly what my dad had done, tear my shoes off and throw my beat up little feets in the icy waters. Boy, was my dad smart! It felt *so* good.

The road from Lone Pine to Whitney Portal looks like something out of an old western. Well, actually, it *is* something out of an old western. A reddish rock formation, known as Alabama Hills, lies on the north side of the road and is where many an old movie was filmed. I kept eyeing those hills, half expecting the Lone Ranger to pop out at any moment and give me a *damn ride* to Lone Pine.

Shawn, like a little cartoon, had a light bulb go off somewhere among those hills.

"Guys! You know what we *should* do?!"

Josh slowed his pace and turned to look at my fiancé, who was growing increasingly giddy as his idea began to take hold of him.

"We should go into Lone Pine, belly up to the bar with Jim and tell our story! SANDWALKERS!!" he cried.

"Sandwalkers!" had become our war cry whenever the situation called for it, which was quite often. Dad had coined the term forty-three years

The blister doesn't fall far from the father.

ago, loosely borrowing and converting it from an 1849 wagon train that had been stranded in Death Valley and whose members barely made it out alive. I had then adapted Dad's term to better describe us as the "Sand-walkers: Second Edition." We all lovingly called him the *OG Sandwalker*, short for "original." Us Second Editioners completely revered the guy that had done this forty-three years ago without the technology, amenities, and guidance from an OG.

Anyway, Josh and I stared at Shawn, who had stars in his eyes and suds on his mind. I didn't *hate* the idea. It was warm out, my knee hurt pretty darn bad, and a frosty beer could help to remedy both of those situations. Plus I liked the idea of hanging out with Mom and Dad and taking a break. To be honest, I *always* like the idea of taking a break.

Josh scoffed a little. I mean it was before noon, and we were doing somewhat strenuous physical activity, so beer was the last thing on his mind. He was also trying to keep a good pace because we had many more miles to go that day. Apparently, Shawn had done an effective job planting the seed, though; eventually Josh warmed to the idea. I radioed Dad—he had gotten me a great little portable radio so that we could keep in constant touch should we need anything—and ran the idea past him. Of course, a support party must do whatever it takes to provide said support to his protégés, right? If that meant drinking an ice-cold beer in the middle of the day, why that is just exactly what he would do. With that, he set about driving around Lone Pine in search of a bar where we could "belly up and tell our story."

He was unsuccessful. He radioed back with the bad news that the only bar to look promising was closed. He had pulled on the door handle and everything—no dice. Darn it.

Shawn wouldn't give up on this dream of his, though, and started doing some research on his phone as we walked. Cell service was a luxury. We only had it for that day and wouldn't see it again until the end of The Walk. He made a phone call and found that the bar Dad had checked was now open, apparently having just done so.

See, divine intervention.

The last mile into Lone Pine was an exciting one, being as we had something cold and frosty calling our name. We limped in through the swinging tavern doors (yes, I am serious) of Jake's Saloon. We couldn't have ended up at a more fitting place; Jake's was an old, slightly run down hole-in-the-wall covered in signed dollar bills. We beat our support party

We were feeling something, all right.

to the bar, so we took a seat and pondered the beers on tap. We later learned that my mom had taken a wrong turn and was heading merrily down the highway *south* of Lone Pine while my dad waited for her to pick him up at the Lone Pine Visitor's Center. It took some time for them to straighten that out, even more so than it took for us to walk to Jake's.

By the time Mom and the "OG" had arrived, we had all decided on the same beer, and, as the Knight who guarded the Holy Grail said to Indiana Jones, we had "chosen wisely." The beer was called Acrodectes and was brewed in Bishop at the Mountain Rambler Brewery. I am not sure if it was my fatigue, the heat, the wonderful company around me, or the fact that we were actually doing The Walk, but that was the best damn beer I have ever had.

Sadly, Shawn's grand scheme to tell everyone in the bar our story didn't quite pan out. We were the only patrons, and the bartender was totally uninterested and impolite to boot. She wouldn't even let us add a signed dollar to their collection on the wall. It truly didn't matter though; we had a blast. Mom and Josh had to practically tear Dad, Shawn, and I away from the bar—all three of us were ready to order a second. I don't think we would have walked another mile that day had I got my little swollen paws on another Acrodectes.

Thanks, Jake, what an amazing memory. We won't soon forget it.

A LITTLE HELP FROM JAKE

—Jim—

We were up before dawn again the next morning, but because it was far beyond 1:50 a.m. it felt almost like sleeping in. At first light we were on our way up the mountain in Josh's Subaru, with Josh as the driving instructor and me piloting the discombobulating beast, while the Sandwalkers sat as passengers nervously holding their abbreviated packs in their laps, no doubt wishing they were parachutes. When we arrived—safely, I might add—at Whitney Portal I dropped them off at the exact point they'd stopped walking last night, so they'd not miss anything. With the exception of Withanee's legs, which looked a little bent, they appeared to be in fine shape and good spirits.

Then I drove back down by myself, trying to figure out just how this car-of-the-future downshifted, recalling the good old days when scenery crept by on mole-skinned foot. It was my most fervent hope that, if I survived, this would be the last time I ever traveled Whitney Portal Road.

When I got back to camp the first thing I did in the breaking daylight—after I figured out how to shut down the Subaru, that is—was to peek under the 4Runner. The ground beneath was surprisingly clean with no discernable engine parts laying around and no oil pooling in the pine needles, so I went ahead and opened the hood. Val had joined me by then so after we ruled out any blindingly obvious damage we had two sets of eyes carefully looking for anything at all untoward or out of place.

Nothing. Zip. Nada. Same old dirty engine it'd always been.

It was a quart low on oil which was easily remedied, and when I cranked it up it turned right over. The engine ran as smooth as ever and the tailpipe wasn't spewing out any blue smoke, although it looked awful sooty as did the rear bumper. I now had high hopes I could at least drive it into Lone Pine, which was considerably more than we'd expected. Puzzling though. Very puzzling.

The hikers reached camp about an hour later, bringing their appetites with them. It took maybe ten minutes to break down camp and have everything packed up, after which Val served scrambled eggs with cheese, sausage, toast, and orange juice. Who needs a five-star restaurant when you have the kitchen amenities provided in a 25-foot motor home, I always say. And a Val, you'll need a Val to go with it, or it's peanut butter sandwiches.

Kelly Harper was having a hard time tearing herself away, as we all knew she would. Kelly was on the engine crew where Withanee was assigned when she first joined the Forest Service firefighters a few years back, and the two became fast friends after Kelly took her under her wing. They are polar opposites in political respects, and it's heartening to see how they've swept all that stuff aside and remain steadfast in their friendship. It's nice to watch the divisiveness splitting this country fall so agreeably flat on its ugly face. Perhaps we could all take a page out of that book.

And although Kelly didn't walk any farther than Lone Pine Campground, she could at least carry with her the title of honorary Sandwalker with a capital S for her one-day round trip to the summit of Mt. Whitney. If ever she were to complete the Sandwalker title she'd have to fill in the letters between "S" and "er"—the "andwalk" part—requiring her to walk and walk and walk until she reached Death Valley.

The now-depleted Second Edition shouldered their packs and headed out to Lone Pine, Withanee already limping noticeably with a swollen knee just as her father had forty-three years ago. All we could do was wrap it with what was state-of-the-art treatment four decades ago and apparently still today—the Ace bandage. That speedy downhill from the summit of Whitney is a real knee-killer, I'll tell you.

I gingerly drove the 4Runner out of the campground with Val following in the Subaru watching for tailpipe smoke and any parts dropping away. We were in contact with each other and with the walkers via handheld radios, and as we motored past them I had two separate witness statements that the 4Runner was visually doing just fine. Additionally, third gear was providing engine braking just like nothing had happened yesterday.

Things were getting curiouser and curiouser, but everything was running so well we went right through Lone Pine and parked the 4Runner a couple miles out of town in the Forest Service parking lot, after which we repeated the trip ferrying the Mini Winnie over. First though, Val followed as I drove Winnie down to an RV park several miles to the south of town, where we used the dump station and refilled everything.

The mistake I made was to drive away while Val was still in the mini-market getting goodies. When I got back to the Forest Service parking lot she wasn't in sight even after I'd been sitting there for awhile. Pretty soon the walkie-talkie crackled and it was Val, asking if she should have turned right when she exited the RV park, the question itself suggesting she'd gone the wrong direction. It took a half hour or so to get all that sorted out, and in the meantime I heard from our hikers; they'd had a change of plans also.

So, with Val driving the Subaru we returned to Lone Pine to meet the Sandwalkers (Second Edition), as requested, at Jake's Saloon.

Jake's Saloon?

Why, yes. It was my future son-in-law's idea, you see. Both he and Josh were toting these small electronic whizzies that not only showed where you were on a little pixel map but also listed the whereabouts of various concerns in the area, one of which happened to be Jake's Saloon. It was only a block off their planned route, and morale was a little flimsy at that point, and since they had to take a break *some*where...

I would point out here that the original Sandwalkers had stopped in Lone Pine too, at a burger joint somewhere along the road that was there no longer, so while we'd been stuck with a cheeseburger and milkshake, the new bunch had what I considered to be a much-improved idea; since they were about to enter the notoriously hot Mojave Desert, why not take their break in a fan-cooled saloon rather than an oven-heated café?

No contest there.

I might add that Jake's Saloon in Lone Pine offers an India Pale Ale on tap that is exceptionally refreshing, and one glass of it got us up and going again in much better spirits (har-de-har). I insisted on paying for it of course, but not so strenuously that I actually did.

As an aside, the original support party for the original Sandwalkers had, while trying to cool off a bit (the twin VW vans they were using had no air conditioning) adopted a saloon in Lone Pine called Mr. Ed's.

I supposed the name was in reference to the television talking horse by that name, and I may have once even seen him in there. The staff at Mr. Ed's had gotten so interested in the stories of our trek that they had chipped in and presented us with a small sterling silver trophy with our names engraved on it after The Walk was over.

In contrast the barkeep in Jake's Saloon had no such interest at all this time around, which was fortuitous I think—I had no desire to glimpse another talking horse, trophy or not.

IF THE HEAT DON'T GET YA, THE TRAFFIC WILL

— *Withanee* —

I can't speak for everyone else, but I came out those swingin' saloon doors with a grin on my face. That 8 percent manna from which I had partaken had given me a boost, that's for sure. We promised to meet Mom and Dad down the road a couple of miles, at the junction of highway 395 and 136, where Mom would have lunch waiting for us. My knee hurt about 8 percent less, and we hobbled on down the sidewalks of Lone Pine, my trekking poles clickity-clicking a great little show tune.

Ok, so I may have had a slight buzz.

Time ambled by and soon-ish we were on the outskirts of town and walking past the very small Lone Pine airport. I stopped to take a quick photo to send to my Aunt Jean—my dad's sister. Forty-three years ago, when my dad had finished The Walk, his parents, my Aunt Jean, and Uncle Jim flew into that very airport to surprise him. I love to hear them both tell of it, Jean being absolutely terrified of airplanes, yet bouncing on down from Oregon in a tiny little charter death trap. My dad, so out of it from his journey, barely even registered they were there, and it didn't really hit him until after they had gone. I had always thought that a little strange but can fully understand and appreciate that kind of exhaustion, nay, delirium now.

Before I knew it, we could see the Minnie Winnie parked at the junction and it was growing larger by the second. Time never went fast on that walk, so I know that had to be the beer happily sloshing around, propelling me forward. We climbed up into the motor home and rested our bones while Mom fixed us up some grilled cheese sandwiches.

By then, I had gotten into a routine of unwrapping and icing my knee

Déjà vu.

at every stop where we met our support party. My mother, God bless her soul, was constantly restocking the Minnie Winnie with ice packs and ace bandages. In fact, she completely bought out Lone Pine's little store of them and my knee was ever so grateful. It had begun to swell and hate me more with each step. Josh had developed a gigantic blister on the bottom of his foot, which would later somehow form another blister on top of that blister, and if you ever thought that wasn't possible, you'd be wrong.

Shawn remained utterly unfazed.

Ice bag off, ace bandage on, snacks resupplied. We took a quick picture in front of a sign similar to what Dad's crew took back in '74. It wasn't the exact same sign. This one had obviously replaced it and it was just a normal road sign that listed the distances. It gave one of our destinations along the way to the lowest point, Panamint Springs, 47 miles. Well shoot, we'd be there in no time.

We headed out into Owen's Valley. Every once in a while I would turn to glance back at Mt. Whitney. That old gal, she sure changed my life. It was staggering to think that the peak was 10,000 feet above where we now walked. *10,000 feet!* Just yesterday, I had stood two vertical miles above this road I now limped along. That thought gave me encouragement like a soft pat on the back at how far we had come. Maybe this actually *was* possible. Maybe.

For some reason, random terms and phrases from Dad's book kept floating through my mind. "Into the Valley of Owens" was one chapter title of his that stuck with me. As we walked and I looked around the valley, I kept turning that phrase over and over in my tired mind. It reminded me of "The Charge of the Light Brigade" by Tennyson, only my version went more like: "Into the Valley of Death walked the three idiots... Theirs is not to reason why; theirs is to do or die. Into the Valley of Death walked the three idiots."

Walking next to the highway is not something I recommend. First off, there wasn't much of a shoulder, probably because no one in their right minds would think about walking here, so what would be the point? Cars zoomed by so fast their wind rattled me and I could taste their exhaust. Some moved over for us, some didn't, and Shawn scolded me more than a few times about not jumping over into the brush when we saw one coming.

Poor guy. I got his point, but for one, I couldn't *jump* to save my life; my legs hadn't worked right since we started down Mt. Whitney. Two, the brush was pokey, and I didn't want to get stickers in my socks. I know I was starting to worry him though, if a particularly distracted driver came too close I could easily teeter over and get smushed like the PB&J sandwich that had been in the bottom of my pack for the past two days. The concern was really starting to show on his face, so I agreed to try. It was so much work, trying to step aside for those stupid cars on my stupid battered legs that were failing me more by the mile. Grrrr.

The beer was definitely wearing off.

AT LEAST IT AIN'T STEEP

—Jim—

Some Gatorade and a couple of grilled cheese sandwiches later and they started east along the highway again, after posing next to a highway mileage sign that had replaced the one that stood there in '74. Another noticeable difference in the scenery, perhaps the most glaring, was the Visitors Center itself. That was open desert when we'd come through way back then. We had unfolded our chairs and relaxed on a graveled turnout beneath a few well-placed shade trees at the junction of the highways. But time, much like our Sandwalkers, marched on with very little notice, if you didn't count the Visitor's Center.

We considered having a mechanic in Lone Pine check the 4Runner, but it's been my experience that unless you can show them a symptom or two they're going to shrug you off, so we decided we'd continue on and see if anything developed. If nothing else we'd be a few miles closer to home, and since tow trucks charge by the mile we might at least save a few bucks.

I led in the 4Runner again and we found an open area 4 or 5 miles down the road suitable to get the motor home well off the highway. Before riding back in the Subaru I again inspected the 4Runner and again found nothing apparent out of whack. Perhaps it was because the roads we were using today were much easier on the engine, but that seemed a weak explanation for what had certainly appeared to be a catastrophic failure. I thought it far more likely that God sometimes wears mechanic's coveralls.

Still somewhat baffled we went ahead and retrieved the motor home and set up camp, after which I climbed the access ladder onto the roof to watch the Second Edition approach through binoculars. My vantage point was much more enjoyable than the one they had, a condition I could swear to in a court of law without a hint of perjury, having been there and done that. This portion of the highway was, like most, slightly domed for drainage, so the shoulders have a barely perceptible outward slant. Since you have to stay on the shoulder to avoid stumbling through heavy brush alongside, that minor slant when sprinkled with loose gravel makes for unstable footing—no slight drawback if your knees and ankles and feet are already hurting.

When we walked it in '74 the wind was fiercely building itself into a sandstorm which was an added aggravation, but these guys were doing in two days what had taken us three, so their suffering was no doubt at least equal to ours. However, once misery gets beyond a certain point the degree of said misery becomes irrelevant, and the only thing that keeps you going is the sure and certain knowledge that once this part is over things will start getting better.

Sad to say, if you're walking from Mt. Whitney to Death Valley you can't get any more delusional than that.

From the roof of the motor home I also had an uncluttered view of the brush-lined Owens River threading its way down the valley from right to left. Unless it rained heavily the river would be the last body of water the Sandwalkers (Second Edition) would see this trip. It used to be a real river filling up Owens Lake, which now showed itself as a salt flat away to the south, but in 1974 the Owens River was but a series of shallow pools held together by mere trickles. On this day it looked much healthier than it had back then, and that might have been my faded memories dancing around, but maybe not; perhaps the Owens River had been granted at least a partial respite from its diversion.

It's hard to picture this part of the Mojave as a farming community with a broad lake plied by a sternwheeler, like the ones seen on Mark Twain's Mississippi, but the history books say it was indeed that, and more, fed by snowmelt from the towering Sierra Nevada Mountains nearby. That came to an end at the turn of the twentieth century when a canal was trenched along the foothills to carry that snowmelt off to up-and-coming Los Angeles. The Mojave Desert didn't lose any time claiming what was left over, resulting in a lot less greenery in this part of the country. And the fishing wasn't very good after that either.

A small cement bridge spans the shrunken riverbed, and in 1974 we had leaned our packs against the guardrail and scooted down to soak our feet in a stagnant and undoubtedly toxic pool, as everything in California had long since been officially determined to cause cancer. Undeterred, it had been a blessed relief to both Ken and I because of our blisters, and we were also sheltered from the windstorm building up that long-ago miserable day, at least for a few moments.

From the top of the motor home I could see the "new" Sandwalkers coming through my binoculars. They were still quite a distance from the bridge but they were striding right along except for Withanee, who was hobbling. Like father like daughter I guess; apparently history does indeed repeat itself.

I climbed down off the roof using the handy built-in rungs on the rear end—which must have been designed with gymnasts in mind—and went about setting up camp. That really didn't amount to much, and since Val was somehow getting dinner going without me I circled the vehicles so the wind would be somewhat broken no matter the direction, if indeed it came up at all. I also set up the folding chairs, spending more than a few minutes making sure they were comfortable and would hold steady for at least 15 or 20 minutes. Each. These sort of patient determinations have always been my blissful strong point.

While waiting for the new bunch I sat there and gazed around, thinking it was actually a pretty campsite with the mountains for a backdrop on all sides. I didn't see that stuff during our original trek, because even if I'd cared to look a sandstorm had hung a curtain in front of everything more than a block away. I did recall losing our thank-goodness-it-wasn't-patented canvas sunshade we'd invented to string between the twin VW microbuses our support party had used. Gary had disappeared into the blowing sand chasing it as it sailed out of sight, and returned a bit later with nothing more than a handful of seashells to show for his effort. Even at that it was hands down the best trade any of us made on that trip, as the sunshade—even when deployed for practice in the parking lot of the paper mill—was a lot more trouble than it was worth. Out of all the useless inventions we'd come up with for the original walk, this one was clearly the headliner.

The new batch of Sandwalkers made it into camp just before sunset, and they certainly would have seemed awfully tired to anyone who hasn't walked in their shoes. To me they looked incredibly fit and even a bit jolly. Well, except for my daughter, who didn't. Her knee was swollen and her feet were blistered, and I felt just terrible, because she was doing a very passable imitation of her father forty-three years ago. And it wasn't that

Josh and Shawn weren't feeling the effects because they were; it's just that Withanee was my daughter and I was supposed to shield her from dumb stuff like this. Or something.

I couldn't help but notice her brother Josh had become the designated leader much like Glenn Burnett had long ago; he just ended up in front naturally. Josh, being the oldest of the new bunch, was also pretty darn fit from the Spartan competitions he regularly engaged in. They ran miles of obstacle courses that would take the starch out of Arnold Schwarzenegger, and they did it willingly, unlike we who endured things like that in military boot camp. He was also very protective of his little sister, and I often regret not spending more time with him and his brother Jedediah, who was a wildland firefighter like Shawn and Withanee. After Withanee was born I became focused on her and passed up a chance to be a real stepfather to the boys. Another not-very-good choice, I suppose, although With and I did have a great time, and I enjoyed every single minute with her, so it's kind of difficult to wish for anything that might have detracted from that. Still, whenever I'm around my stepsons there is that lingering hollowness.

Shawn I'd known for the past couple of years, and from the very first time I met him I liked him, which is pretty rare, at least for me. At the time they lived up at Lake Tahoe, Shawn a member of the Black Mountain Hotshots and Withanee serving on an engine based out of Markleeville. That was an eight-hour drive from where Val and I lived in Tecopa and later Pahrump, in good weather that is, so we didn't see them very often, but when we did we had a great time. Shawn jumped right in to metal detecting and prospecting and anything else we came up with, so it did enter my mind that they'd make a great married couple. In support of that, well, there's the Fourth of July proving ground; you just can't go wrong with a guy who loves bottle rockets.

We all had a surprisingly enjoyable evening at the Dolomite Loop Road, sitting around with a cold brew or two while the walkers soaked their aching feet in tubs of water and Epsom salts. Val served up a great dinner, after which Shawn insisted I read a chapter out of my book describing the next day's miseries. I was conflicted about that, hoping they might get a pointer or two out of it but at the same time fearing I'd make more of an idiot of myself than I'd already proven to be. It was, after all, my fault my daughter wanted to do this, but I could at least take comfort in the fact that it was her who brought everyone else into it. Shawn and Josh and Kelly were all attributable to Withanee, although they were so willing you wouldn't even guess that they'd been shanghied.

Val was a different kettle of fish; when she heard what was being bandied about—this rewalk of the Mt. Whitney to Death Valley thing—she was adamantly against leading a support party.

She wanted to be one of the walkers.

What are you going to do with a girl like that? I shouldn't have been surprised; in 1999, on the twenty-fifth anniversary of The Walk, Val and I drove to Death Valley in hopes that the other three original Sandwalkers would make good on a pledge to meet at Devil's Golf Course to celebrate the day we finished a quarter of a century earlier. I hadn't been in touch with any of them for at least twenty of those years, so I really wasn't that surprised when nobody showed, but Val wanted to go on to Mt. Whitney and take a look at the entire route. So on we went. She was fascinated with the sheer vastness of The Walk and when we reached Whitney Portal, where the trailhead to the summit begins, she took off up the trail. More on that at the end of this book, but it took a while to get her turned around. It was several years later when we asked her to head up the support party for the Second Edition, and because of that 1999 trip I wasn't surprised when she said no, she wanted to join the walking crew. It took a lot of persuading, but she finally relented and a darn good thing too, because without her the support party wouldn't have offered much support, in which case The Walk could not even be considered. It was a happy, happy day when she finally caved in, sort of; after that there wasn't any graceful way out of it. But for the entire trip she'd get that wistful gaze in her eyes every time she saw them walking.

In 1974, somewhere around where I now laid my head on my lumpy motor home pillow, I'm sure I had some pre-sleep thoughts trying to figure out how in blazes I'd ended up out here.

In 2017 the same thing happened. Deja vu repeated again once more, eh?

I MIGHT JUST KEELER OVER

— *Withanee* —

We finally detoured off the main highway onto Dolomite Loop—an old side road consisting of broken up asphalt and zero traffic. Thank God. I was getting irritable. Unbridled pain has a way of making a person grumpy, and I couldn't wait to finish our 17-mile day.

The Second Edition Sandwalkers came hobbling into camp rewarded by our support party's applause, high-fives, and cold beers at the ready. We retreated to our comfy lawn chairs and enjoyed an incredible sunset. Mom also had little tubs she had filled with hot water and Epsom salt to soak our aching feet in.

Ahh, all was right in the world at the end of day two.

My feeling of total contentment was short lived though, and I had myself another miserable night's sleep. Too tired to set up all three tents, we joined forces to set up the biggest one and piled on in. That night the wind howled, the tent flapped against my head, and every inch of me ached. Coyotes howled their annoying ditty so loud and relentless that if this wasn't California, I would have crawled out of the tent and shot them. But it was, and God knows I didn't want to go to jail, though the rest I might find there made it somewhat tempting.

This went on all night long. All. Night. Long.

Poor Shawn had felt a cold coming on the morning we left home and it had been hitting its peak for the last couple of days. He is so tough that he never complained about it, and most times I forgot he was sick. That night though, I could hear him sniffling miserably, and I felt so bad for him. On the other side of me, my big brother was snoring like a freight train.

Snore, flap, throb, howl, sniffle.

I finally learned my lesson that night and didn't use a tent for the rest of the trip.

Day three dawned and the bandaging began. The pain was almost unbearable as the guys helped me slide into my pack. There were so many times I thought, "Nope. This is it. It can't get worse than this. Only up from here, Andersen!" Just to be proved wrong later in the day, then again the next mile, and the next morning after that. I figured the repetitiveness of it all would mean my body would adapt and the aches would start to fade, but every day there was something new. My knee was still by far my biggest adversary, but somewhere around the second day I began to develop blisters. *Boy, are they fun.*

Dad had regaled me with the horrors of the pain he endured for that June week in 1974, and it's not like I hadn't believed him. I had. My dad has a way of describing things that make them so perfectly clear (as I'm sure you will find out in this book) that you will swear later that you were there, too. But he also gave me a small snippet of hope in the form of comparison: though we were both exactly thirty years old when we made this trek, Dad was sure I was in far better shape than he had been. I was a firefighter for heaven's sake. I clung to that hope in the months and final days leading up to The Walk. It hadn't mattered though; apparently my body had forgotten what I did for a living the first moment I stepped onto the trailhead at Whitney Portal. The one thing fire did prepare me for was the mental aspect and there is something to be said for that. Dad had that too though, that mind's pit bull jaw strength to bite onto an idea and be totally unable to let it go. In all, I'd say Dad and I were pretty evenly matched.

Which really was the whole point, wasn't it? To recreate Dad's trip exactly, it was only fair that I was in this much pain but kept going anyway. So, once I got somewhat upright in my pack of the morning of day three, I tucked my head like a determined little turtle, with about the same speed, and went on.

We followed Dolomite Loop until it came back out to meet Highway 136.

Great.

I had not the wherewithal to dodge traffic that morning, and my fellow Sandwalkers had gotten pretty good at reading me by then, so they knew without me having to grunt a peep. Consulting their phone maps and each other, they found a potential new route in which we could veer off somewhat parallel to the highway, giving us distance from the speeding traffic along another old and broken road in which no one drove. I came to love these old roads and new routes they conjured up, this one especially. After a few hours, we came to what Sandwalkers yearn for: *sand.*

The direct correlation of terrain and my happiness throughout the entire walk was astounding. Never having noticed the ground in any manner before, I came to learn just exactly how influential it is on an aching body. Even walking alongside a highway where the shoulder looks flat and smooth, it is anything but. Hard ground, a slight unevenness, a sharp rock every now and again, all things that made a considerable difference on the level of pain I was experiencing. And the pain wasn't confined to my feet. Like the old tune "Dem Bones," whenever I took a step I felt it travel in jolts up the length of my body. It perhaps lasted a mini-second, but what I felt was:

> *The foot bone's connected to the ankle bone [ouch],*
> *The ankle bone's connected to the shin bone,*
> *The shin bone's connected to the knee bone [uumph],*
> *The knee bone's connected to the thigh bone,*
> *The thigh bone's connected to the hip bone [arg]*

And of course, it keeps going up your back and into your brain. I swear, even my fingernails hurt. I was hyper aware of the fact it was going to do that for the next hundred or so miles and that thought was enough to make me cry. I did find two moments of this terrain-pain relief; one on the very last day in the form of a short-lived salt creek and the other in this very sand we discovered on day three.

Sliding my feet through the grains of sweet relief, I managed a cheer of joy. A couple miles in this stuff really made my heart sing. We saw our little support party on the highway, and I just had to radio in with my news.

"Dad! We found sand!"

"All right Withy! Way to go! SANDWALKERS!"

Since we didn't need any support at the moment other than the cheers he had already provided, Dad moved the motor home down the road where we would eventually rendezvous for lunch in the town of Keeler. I use the word *town* loosely; I had been fantasizing of a shimmering oasis with perhaps another bar to visit and take the edge off the pain. I made the mistake of voicing this to my teammates, whose mouths began watering at the thought of another frosty mug. I was horribly wrong. Keeler is a handful of mobile homes tossed haphazardly together in the middle of the desert. Disappointed, hot, and hungry, we stumbled into the motor home for our waiting lunch. Except, our lunch wasn't waiting.

"Wait, where's Mom?"

Dad shrugged his shoulders, looking somewhat sheepish. Well, that was curious.

As it turns out, she had gone back to Lone Pine for more supplies that morning but had yet to return. Somehow she had gotten confused and had taken (or tried to take) Dolomite Loop Road near where we had camped the night before. After finding that to be too rough she turned around and went back toward the highway. The highway runs in a straight line from Lone Pine to Keeler, so had she just stayed straight she would have been fine, but my mom is a Black Belt in getting lost (see Jake's Saloon incident) and I absolutely love her for it. The few spare minutes we had before she came screeching into Keeler in a cloud of dust gave me some time to ice my knees and rest my miserable body. For that, I am eternally grateful.

WHEN KEELER BECOMES THE HIGHLIGHT OF YOUR DAY . . .

—Jim—

We were up early again just as first light was breaking above the Coso Mountains to the east. It seemed slightly chilly, which I found unnerving; I was never chilled on the original walk after we left Mt. Whitney behind, probably because the Mojave Desert had just welcomed in summer at that time. This trip, on the other hand, had just welcomed in autumn. But in the Grand Mojave autumn usually isn't readily distinguishable from summer. Cactus needles aren't deciduous you know, they don't shimmer bright red and yellow and float to the ground like leaves and there isn't any frost on the pumpkins around here. But there is, occasionally, a chill, at least to us now-practicing southern desert people.

I mean it had to be, like, an arctic 65 out there.

I fired up the generator so "we" could make coffee and breakfast and which also worked really well as an alarm clock to any sleep kapeeps in the area. Of which there were at least three, coming through the door even as "we" poured coffee (from here on out I'll leave the quotation marks out from around "we," as it must be obvious that I was awful busy with other stuff). Other stuff would include checking Josh's blister upon blister on the ball of his right foot. A blister on the ball of your foot was a new one to me, and I had so many blisters on the original walk that I almost had a pair of socks made out of moleskin. We tried lancing it with no success and finally hoped to corral it with a huge piece of moleskin, which was pretty darned brilliant but wouldn't stay on long enough to make much difference. Shawn wasn't feeling well, had a cold or some misery like that, but insisted he'd be just fine as soon as he finished his coffee. Other than a little stiffness, he looked unfazed.

And then there was Withanee. Her right knee was swollen to the size of a softball, but other than wrapping it with an Ace bandage there was no further medical solution available. I knew that from my vast storehouse of experience wherein Mt. Whitney had victimized me in the same fashion.

Happily, she didn't have any Josh-like spectacular blisters at the moment, but by the red welts you could tell she was working on it. We applied moleskin as needed. As much as I tried not to, I couldn't help but wince right along with her.

Val whipped up a breakfast of cheese omelets, sausage, toast, and orange juice, further enshrining herself firmly into the Sandwalker Hall of Fame. With a smile and a wave the Second Edition then walked, sort of, off into their third day. Val and I watched until they dwindled into the distance, and then we hugged each other and went about packing up. You get really good at that after a while.

On this day Val and I elected to take the Minnie Winnie to the RV station together, before we leapfrogged the other vehicles toward tonight's campsite. Because there were five of us dependent on the resources of the motor home, it was apparent we'd have to replenish supplies and dump the holding tanks daily, which was going to require a little juggling; there were only three RV stations available to us, one 10 miles south of Lone Pine, one at Panamint Springs, and one at Furnace Creek. Today would be our last visit to the one near Lone Pine, and since there wasn't any reason to take two vehicles we decided we'd enjoy the trip together.

We returned a couple of hours later and had just shut off the engine when Val noticed she'd missed an item on her shopping list, so she decided she'd take Josh's Subaru back to Lone Pine while I moved the Minnie Winnie to Keeler, where we planned to meet the Second Edition for lunch. So off she went in one direction while I motored away in another.

Funny how our minds work; you'd think one of us would have recalled Val's exceptional ability to get lost when left to her own devices like that.

I followed in the walker's footsteps down Dolomite Loop until it rejoined Highway 136 some 4 miles distant, then turned east toward Keeler. Unbeknownst to me, our Sandwalkers had done the same thing we'd done all those many years before; they'd left the highway and had angled off across the desert where the walking was less stressful. Not that it would be easy; there would be no easy walking for the Second Edition until this trip was over and in the books. I knew that from personal experience, and being in the support party instead of *out there* was surreal and sometimes disorienting in a hazy sort of manner. . . . I jumped when the walkie-talkie squelched, roused out of my daydreaming by my daughter's voice.

"Hey Dad, can you hear me?"

There was no other traffic anywhere in sight, which was a good thing. I glanced around and slowed the Minnie Winnie way down while fumbling with the handheld before replying.

"Yes. Yes I hear you. Whereabouts are you?"

She said they were off to my right, walking through cushioning sand for a pleasant change, then hollered out, in unison; *"Sandwalkers!"* I probably could have heard them without the radio.

There was a well-used dirt road crossing the highway, and I turned onto it and pulled over. It took a couple minutes to find them in my binoculars. They were maybe a mile distant, waving their walking sticks and looking surprisingly fit. I honked back and when they asked how far it was to Keeler I had to admit I didn't know, perhaps an hour for them—a few minutes for me. They said they'd meet us there for lunch as planned. When they asked if Val was with me I told them she was probably already at Keeler.

Knowing Val had driven off without a guide I don't know why I thought she could find Keeler. Sure enough, it quickly became apparent that Val hadn't. I drove around the few blocks that comprised Keeler and there wasn't a black Subaru hiding anywhere.

Oh, my.

Well surely she'd be along before the walkers got there, so I parked in the turnout right next to the highway so she couldn't go by without my seeing her. Val also had a walkie-talkie with her but I didn't want to babble her absence over the airwaves, fearing our daughter would surely overhear. That wouldn't do anybody any good, and might indeed cause more problems than it solved. No, surely the wisest course would be to just sit there and make sure Val didn't go whistling by unnoticed.

She didn't.

When the walkers arrived Val was still AWOL, and when Withanee opened the motor home door I, like Lucy Arnaz, had some 'splainin' to do. I was never very good at explaining stuff like that and I may have lowered the bar even a bit more this time, as it didn't go very well.

"*Daaad!!*" my daughter said in the tone I used to use when she did something stupid growing up. I suppose I had it coming but I did appreciate Josh and Shawn coming to my verbal rescue. I think the main thing, other than misplacing her mother, was that lunch hadn't been made, so I started to correct that. Bologna and cheese sandwiches had always been a staple of mine, and as I was whipping up a right nice repast the cavalry finally arrived in the form of Val.

Her excuse? She'd missed the Highway 136 turnoff coming out of Lone Pine and had gone "quite a ways" down the road before she noticed and turned around. When she found herself back in Lone Pine she turned around again and finally got back on highway 136, where she reflexively returned to our Dolomite campsite, the only inhabitant now being Yoda. Oops. But instead of turning left toward Keeler when she returned to the highway she turned right and ended up retracing her earlier steps to Lone Pine yet again—for the third time—before turning around and heading in what would finally turn out to be the right route to Keeler.

You just have to stand in awe of a gift like that.

I THINK I'LL JUST STAY HERE AND DRINK

— *Withanee* —

After a bologna lunch only a dad could make, I got the gumption to strap a GoPro camera on my head to get some pictures of the second half of the day. Here is something really odd about The Walk: Back up on Mt. Whitney, just as the sun was about to peek its way through the darkness, Josh had asked me to hook his GoPro on one of the straps of his pack and set it to the time lapse setting. I did, and waited to make sure I saw the red light flash every thirty seconds, signaling that it was *indeed* taking time lapse photos. He wore that sucker all the way to the top, where he found his battery dead—which was to be expected in that amount of time. As we started back down Whitney, he and I decided I should use my own GoPro to get a time lapse of the journey back, rounding out our day with plenty of photos. Back at camp that night, we were excited to look at the footage of our incredible day. However, when we pressed "play" there was not a single photo on either one of our cameras.

Strange.

So, I thought I'd try again, this time with Dad's GoPro (we really are a camera family), because there's no way three cameras would malfunction on the same trip, right?

Wrong. I walked the next few miles looking like a plumed quail for absolutely nothing. When Dad tried to look at the photos I had taken with his camera it too came up empty. I can't make this stuff up. It was like we were in the Bermuda triangle of electronics. This book wouldn't make a very good advertisement for GoPros, though I have never had trouble with them before or since.

Anyway, we trudged back out and had no other choice this time but to

Two words: cargo koozies.

walk along the highway. I was feeling *rough,* and it became quickly clear that Josh wouldn't be able to keep at my slow pace. Off he went. Shawn, of course, stayed with me as I hobbled along using my trekking poles as crutches. We had only gone a couple of miles when I had had enough.

"I can't do this, my knee is killing me." I whined.

But Shawn didn't give up on me, a trait that I hope he carries through our entire marriage, and just as I began to whine again, the rest of my support party came toodling on down the highway behind us. Next thing I knew, Dad had the motor home pulled over on the shoulder and was handing us Gatorade and an ice-cold beer.

Beer. If you haven't sensed a recurring theme yet, I'll go ahead and spell it out now. I will also take this opportunity to tell you something my very wise, seventy-three-year-old father taught me: deep cargo pants pockets make excellent beer holders.

That image will forever last in my memory. It was so awesome. I could have easily clambered up in that motor home and drunk beers with Dad all day. But alas, onward dear Sandwalkers. Josh again caught his stride and broke through the wall that I kept smacking into. We all were amused by this later, because Josh had got this walker's high or whatever you want to call it in the exact same spot that my dad did. In fact, they even have similar photos. . . .

Like father, like stepson.

Look at those grinning fools. About thirty minutes later, Shawn and I came in, looking nothing like the photos above.

At this point, we plopped into the lawn chairs our wonderful support party had waiting for us. This is a specific moment during The Walk that I remember looking over at my dad, who had his photo album out and was pointing out something yonder to Josh, and I simply stared at him in awe. How on earth did he *do* this?

I wanted this painful day to be over and the suds to be flowing aplenty, but we had reached an important decision-making point. We could camp in the spot we were in, which is exactly where the OG Sandwalkers had camped so many years before, or push on another few miles to set us up

Fighting to stay upright.

better for the next day. The next day. *Canyon Day*. Dad's recount about Canyon Day had terrified me, which I would come to find out didn't even compare to the real nightmare. We knew that we had to continue as far as we could to lessen the beating. At least, that is what they kept telling me. I would have been totally satisfied to lay down in the dirt and die.

With much groaning, we pushed ourselves up and gathered our gear. The plan was for the support party to go on ahead to find us a sufficient campsite further down the road and for us to hobble on to meet them there. I was at a real low point, or at least I thought I was. It turned out it was more of my normal baseline for the duration of this week. As I was busy trying to push myself upright, Shawn picked up his empty beer can and turned toward the motor home with the intent of popping in and throwing it away. As he stepped up into the door frame, however, he got wedged in because of his walking stick he had stowed sideways, ninja turtle style, in his pack. He tried reaching out and pushing forward again, to again get vehemently stopped by the doorframe, arm outstretched, beer can dangling. I don't know if it didn't register in his mind at that point or if he was just determined, but he kept trying, always with the same abrupt result.

My dad absolutely lost control and the next thing I know we were all bent over howling with laughter.

Someone forgot to tell the stick that three's a crowd.

That *damned* stick. I had been totally flabbergasted when Shawn didn't buy any gear for the hike, specifically trekking poles. As it turns out, he had made a very large purchase in that thing that twinkled from my ring finger and wasn't about to spend another dime on this trip—not something that I knew beforehand but now made all the sense in the world. Back at Lone Pine campground, my fella had cut a branch off a tree and used a knife to make notches in the top for his fingers, while my dad supervised. More than once when he reached to hug me I got smacked in the head by that stick. He carried it the entire walk, and it now sits in our living room, watching over us. Don't tell him this, but I love that stupid thing.

Anyhow, it took us all a while to get ourselves back together and stagger back on the highway. I could still hear Dad laughing when he got into the driver's seat of the Minnie Winnie and I smiled in spite of myself. Like the Bible says, a merry heart does good like a medicine, *indeed*.

We knocked out another 2 miles, and just as the sun was dipping behind the mountains, we came into camp for the night, having completed 19.3 miles for the day. The spot Mom and Dad had found was a nice one, with soft dirt with which to dig out a spot to lay in. This was the first night I didn't mess with a tent, just threw a tarp on the ground with my sleeping bag on top. It was the best night sleep I'd had yet.

THE ONLY SMALL WORLD IS AT DISNEYLAND

— Jim —

While our reunited party ate lunch I couldn't help glancing out the window at Keeler. I was last there forty-three-plus years ago but it hadn't changed all that much, although the public phone booth that used to stand at the intersection had long since gone the way of the dodo bird. I'd detoured over to the phone booth that long ago day and made a collect call home, catching my first wife's daughter, Kathy. The *Oakland Tribune* had earlier sent out a reporter to interview us about The Walk and, sure enough, there'd been an article in Sunday's paper, which Kathy read to us over the phone. It was pretty heady stuff, really, for a foursome of paper mill workers. Kathy said it was titled *Four Off on Perilous Trek,* accompanied by a picture of Ken, Glenn, and me above the caption: *With another companion they are trying to climb Mt. Whitney, cross Death Valley.*

Well, well. Any thoughts of quitting this perilous trek that may have been flitting across our minds were gradually quenched as the article gave reference to the "highest peak in the 48 contiguous states" and the "lowest point in the Western Hemisphere" *and the* "roughest and most forbidding terrain on the continent," *and then the grand finale:* "If all goes well, four figures dressed in ghostly white will emerge from the shimmering desert near Badwater in 8 to 10 days."

Well, well. We stared at each other for a few minutes. Those four figures? That's us, now with a destiny to emerge from the shimmering desert near Badwater in eight to ten days. Sure not gonna puppy out now, are we. We turned back to the highway and started walking, no less tired and no less sore but absolutely determined to see this through.

HIKERS GLENN BURNETT, LEFT, KEN OBERG AND LEADER JIM ANDERSEN
With another companion they are trying to climb Mt. Whitney, cross Death Valley

Clipping of the *Oakland Tribune* article, June 16, 1974.

At least for the moment.

As I surveyed the Second Edition Sandwalkers, just then getting ready to shed the motor home and hit the road again, I was scrambling to find some way to give them a morale boost as had been given us by that newspaper article, so as they clambered down into the sunshine I applauded and hollered:

"You guys are doing *great!!* Keep it *up!!*"

It was meant to be congratulatory but somehow came out sounding like a halftime talk to the losing team. I'd have to work on it.

After a few last-minute adjustments to their packs we traded handshakes and hugs and away they went, headed east along the highway one painstaking step at a time; daughter, son, future son-in-law. Hard as it was to believe, Death Valley had never seemed farther away than it did at that moment, even back when I was doing the walking.

Val and I then cleaned and secured everything in Minnie Winnie, locked it up and hopped in the Subaru. Val drove me back to the Dolomite campsite to retrieve the 4Runner, which I then drove to the next original Sandwalker camp, with her following closely while I kept her under close surveillance in the rearview mirror to make sure she didn't wander off. This would become our routine throughout the remainder of The Walk because it worked well, unlike our morning fiasco.

We went breezing past Keeler and a couple miles later honked as we passed the Sandwalkers as well. Another 6 miles and we pulled into the turnout on now-highway 190 where we originally camped in 1974. I hoped to dissuade our walkers from spending the night there, as tomorrow would be Canyon Day and they needed to camp another couple of miles beyond where we were so they had a chance of making it through the canyon before nightfall. We hadn't done that, and we paid for it by having to negotiate the canyon after it faded into darkness. It was awful.

I locked the 4Runner, which was running unbelievably well in spite of its oil explosion back at Mt. Whitney, and Val drove me back to Keeler to get the motor home. When we passed the walkers this time I could see Withanee was having a really hard time staying upright—probably couldn't without the aid of her walking stick—and I yelled at her to hang in there, that we'd return ASAP with goodies for her.

And we did. We retrieved Minnie Winnie, and as soon as we reached them I pulled off on the nearest turnout and waved them over. Val pulled off in the Subaru as well and we set out folding chairs for them complete with cold beer in the armrests. To say this was welcome would be the understatement of the year, and Withy gave me the biggest hug ever—which is saying a lot—before dropping her pack. Josh and Shawn joined right in too, so it was unanimous.

Within a very short period of time—perhaps 20 minutes—The Walkers were recharged and as ready to go as they ever would be, so we helped them gear up and pointed them in the right direction. I knew we'd made the right call when we saw the size of their smiles as they saluted us with their walking sticks. There's never been a finer, more heartfelt tribute than that, so we'd clearly relayed to them a bit of the morale boost that'd been given those many years ago by the newspaper article.

It was another 6 or 7 miles to the place where we original walkers had made camp and where we set up to meet the Second Edition this afternoon, but I had high hopes that they would add a couple more miles to today's total. Again, tomorrow they'd be tackling that horrible, nameless, brutal canyon into Panamint Valley, and if they camped where we did tonight they'd no doubt end up spending a couple hours in the canyon in darkness, like we did. If I could talk them into getting just another mile or two up the road...

Big "if" though. *Huge* "if."

Before we drove back onto the highway I spent some time looking around and thinking back to the day I was one of the walkers. This was a very remarkable day back in 1974, because in addition to the newspaper article I distinctly remember that it was somewhere in this general vicinity that Glenn, who, along with Gary, spent nearly the whole walk far in front of Ken and I, took off like he was on the Keeler Track Team. I couldn't believe his acceleration as he diminished in the manner of the roadrunner sprinting away from Wile E. Coyote. He finally stopped and waited for us to catch up so he could regale us with his Secret Formula; he had hit the "wall" that we'd all heard about and had nothing left, but instead of stopping like we'd been doing he, by force of will, made his foot kick forward as hard as he could, which brought tears to his pain-filled eyes, and then made his other foot kick forward, and again, and again, and again, and all of a sudden he said it quit hurting and away he went like a runaway train.

I didn't believe a word of it but I had actually seen him shrink into the distance with no visible means of propulsion. Had he not stopped and waited for us to catch up I believe we'd have lost him forever. So I tried it, and darned if it didn't work, although I almost passed out before I went into overdrive. I passed Ken and Gary and Glenn and conceivably a couple of Highway Patrolmen with spectacular long sweeping strides, one of which was actually caught on film by our support party when I came charging into camp. Good thing too, because I was never able to repeat it. When I stopped moving that day my whole body seized up like a rusty bolt. By the time my fellow hikers arrived I was nearly in traction paying the piper.

It sure was nice while it lasted though.

I knew the Second Edition was aware of us breaking the wall barrier on this day forty-three years ago because I'd read that chapter of the book to them last night, but I was hoping they wouldn't try to repeat my sprint because once they stopped that would wind up the hiking day and there would be no further campsite in the offing.

Thank heavens they didn't, although Josh gave it a good try and came into camp well in front of the pack. Josh, although he was the oldest at 40, competed regularly in those Spartan events, which are designed to take physical endurance to the next level, but from what I've seen I don't think they break through the wall as much as they ignore it altogether.

Shawn and Withy followed a little later with Shawn doing his level best not to look like he was instrumental in keeping my daughter upright, God bless him.

We dropped into folding chairs again and passed around ice-cold India Pale Ale before I brought out the maps. The Second Edition, all three of them, looked a little bewildered as we clearly had not laid out a campsite. I'm sure I more than once emphasized the need to walk a couple more miles on this particular day due to the harshness of tomorrow's hike, but nothing sinks in quite like reality. This was, after all, where the Original Sandwalkers camped on day three, so since this was a reenactment shouldn't we overnight here?

Um, no. You see, the Original Sandwalkers had learned an awful lesson when they came up short on this day; whatever we left unwalked today was tacked on after nightfall tomorrow, because there was no stopping after the canyon was entered, and the canyon was farther away than we thought it was.

So, were there any options at all?

"Well yes, there is one" I answered. "You can stay here tonight and walk 10 or 12 miles tomorrow, but camp at that point so you'll start into the canyon early the next day and have plenty of time to get the heck out of there in broad daylight. I would have opted for that in 1974 rather than do the dark thing. We were just lucky none of us got injured in there."

"But," Shawn interjected, "that would extend The Walk by a day."

"Probably." I said. Then Val and I went into Minnie Winnie so they could hash it out without us eavesdropping. I waited as long as I could—perhaps 10 minutes—and then came out and raised my eyebrows. They were already standing and getting into their gear. Withy, leaning heavily on her walking stick, gave me a huge grin and a wink.

Q: How do fathers keep their composure at times like these?
A: They don't.

Shawn, bless his wonderful heart, came to my rescue again. He had his handmade walking stick lashed horizontally to his backpack, and when he tried to enter the motor home door to throw his bottle away that stick slammed into the doorframe with enough force to throw him back off the step. Undeterred, he tried it twice more before he figured out something was decidedly wrong. What a great excuse for my tears. Who needs Larry, Curly, and Moe when you got Shawn?

So off they went yet again, Val and I following in our respective vehicles. Our walkers were noticeably slower and less agile than before, which was certainly to be expected but not welcomed.

We backed Minnie Winnie up onto sandy wash exactly one and three-quarter miles from the old campsite and went back for the 4runner, passing the struggling Second Edition both heart-breaking ways. When they finally arrived they were exhausted and sore but in surprisingly good spirits, and we had a restful and enjoyable evening in spite of our struggles.

What a crew.

JOHNNY, JUNE, AND CREEDENCE CLEARWATER

— Withanee —

I awoke at 4:55 a.m.

Immersed in inky darkness, my eyes fluttered open and I took a shallow breath. It wasn't my usual iPhone alarm that had woken me so suddenly, but instead a happy little voice that belonged to my father sweetly asking, "Annnnnnnybody awake?" followed by the strum of a guitar cutting like a machete blade through the blackness.

My dog has fleas.

What?

My foggy brain began to register everything in sequence, beginning with the small RV light off to my right that was acting as a spotlight and illuminating the two people I loved most in this world. My dad sat in a chair with the guitar in his lap with my mom standing next to him: my own little Johnny and June.

My dad used to play the guitar when I was a kid, and although I can't pinpoint when, he had phased it out at one point or another. My uncle also used to play a beauty of a Gibson and now every time I hear even one single strum of a guitar, I am flooded with the warmth of childhood memories and the men I loved. I had since begged my dad to play for me, but the promise of guitar calluses usually dissuaded him, despite my best efforts.

That familiar affection filled my body as I laid on my back and listened to my mom and dad sing "Lookin' for a Reason"—a song significant not only to The Walk but to Canyon Day, specifically. Dad's support party had played this exact same Creedence Clearwater Revival song for the Original Sandwalkers forty-three years earlier, though their 8-track couldn't possibly compare to the live version we were enjoying.

The song, if you haven't heard it, is all about looking for any excuse *at all* not to leave—something I could feel deep in my aching bones. Fogerty's rich voice (and later my dad's) croons about getting caught up in a dream, only to find yourself questioning what the heck you were thinking in the first place.

Huh, sounded familiar.

And yet, you get up and get going anyway. Ole John didn't know it at the time, but that song was written word-for-word for Sandwalkers everywhere. It may be one of CCR's lesser-known tunes, but not to us. The soundtrack of The Walk, "Lookin' for a Reason" still brings with it a smile, and maybe a tear or two.

I folded my arms behind my head as I was serenaded, starting up at the gleaming stars which looked as if they were fighting each other for space in the night sky. There were *so many.* I had the luxury of growing up in a small town with hardly any people and even fewer street lights, so I was comfortably familiar with seeing the sky this way. Yet, for some reason this was something more spectacular than anything I had ever seen. For the umpteenth time this week, I was brought to tears.

Wow.

As it turned out, I think God and my parents both knew we would need this incredible, warm and blissful moment to survive the horrors of the day that lie ahead.

We started back out on the highway that morning just as the sun blessed us with its presence. It was a chilly start to the day, but something about that wakeup call really had us bouncing on down the highway. We continued humming "Lookin' for a Reason" until I grabbed a Bluetooth speaker from my pack and hooked my phone up to play some new tracks to continue our mood. The power of music really is undeniable, and we soon had a funny little conga line going for a couple miles or so as the sun rose on day four. I brought up the rear, I think my dad refers to that as "Tail End Charlie," and I'll tell you what: when Charlie is riddled with incredible knee (and overall body) pain, ol' Charlie can *groove.* It really might have been some of my best moves. Not sure if Shawn and Josh would agree with that, or not.

Like summiting Whitney or that Acrodectes beer before it, the high from our morning serenade eventually wore off, and we continued shuffling down the highway in our line—a little less conga, a little more chain gang, in silence.

There was a part in my dad's book I had all but forgotten until we came upon it that morning in the form of a white cross on the side of the highway. It's funny, you know. I've seen many a' roadside grave but this one gave me all the feels, just as it had my dad so many years before. The cross was tall and strikingly beautiful, with flowers hung where the boards overlapped. At its base lay a long wooden board, with the following information:

Lorenza McKellips—Died In Infancy
Larkin McKellips—4 Years Old

A beautiful reminder that I had it pretty darn good. Blisters be darned.

The date was 1874. My brain turned the words over and over, like a rock kicked off the 99 switchbacks of Mt. Whitney. The McKellips family lost two children. *Two.* In one year. Yes I know, it was the 1800's. I am well aware, due to my extensive time spent playing The Oregon Trail computer game, that things of this nature happened all the time back then. Measles. Typhoid. Diphtheria. Snake venom. Trampled by oxen. Drowned in a river (though I doubt this was the case here). I know all of this was actually fairly common and yet, here I was. One slightly entitled Millennial, griping because my knee hurt. Griping because my $120 shoes were feeling a little tight at the moment. Griping that I had to walk for a week, mind you, followed around by a Minnie Winnie with a never-ending supply of cold beers and delectable eats for my indulgence. And let's not forget, I was *choosing* to do this.

If that isn't enough to make you shed a tear or maybe gag a little bit, I am not sure what will. I did a little bit of both.

The Sandwalkers Second Edition stood in front of that cross for some time, not saying much, but the silence felt heavy. I said a little prayer and thanked God for the chance to have enjoyed thirty years of a privileged life and the ability to be embarking on the adventure of a lifetime. A lifetime that these little McKellips kiddos never got the chance to have.

Ugh.

We quietly shuffled away, maybe a little more grateful for the highway and desolation that sprawled in front of us.

Just a couple miles after leaving camp that morning, Shawn and Josh had already found a potential short cut on their maps. They did this a lot, and every time they would consult their phones and point in the distance I would kind of float out of my body and fly away mentally. I think I was too focused on my pain to care about the map, or the plan, or any other logistics at *any* point during The Walk. Eventually, I would always come to, in harsh realization that they were staring and awaiting my approval of the plan. I would then bob my head in agreement, silently thanking my stars for a glorious minute of leaning on my trekking poles while they did whatever it was they were doing.

Anyway, their newest shortcut was to take a left off of highway 190, (which had been highway 136 but had turned into 190 around Keeler) and onto Talc City Road. I was glad. I really hate highway shoulder walking. Talc City Road was nothing to write home about. Initially broken up asphalt, it turned into a dirt road and led, evidently, to some old talc mines. Interesting enough, but the best part was that this road cut off a little over a mile of the original plan. *Score.*

We popped back out on the highway and crossed it, where our sweet little Minnie Winnie with its sweet little inhabitants sat, waiting expectantly. I was tired already, flat exhausted really, but mentally I was fighting a battle because I knew. I knew that even though we were just over nine miles into the day, and three and a half days into The Walk itself, we weren't to the hard part.

That came next.

'TIL LUNCH DO US PART

— *Jim* —

Val and I were up at 4:45 a.m. the next morning because we had a song we had to sing for our charges as a wake-up call. The reason was that on the original walk our support party had played an eight-track Credence Clearwater tape of a song titled "Lookin' for a Reason" to bring us to wakefulness, which it most certainly did. I'm sure you'd concur if you'd ever used CCR as your rooster in the dawn's early light on the Mojave Desert, so I was determined to do the same for the Second Edition.

However, we had no tape—eight-tracks being obsolete long before 2017 anyway—and we were unable to find a copy of the song anywhere. So just in case we couldn't find one in Lone Pine either, which we didn't, I'd thrown my guitar in the overhead rack when we left home. The song, the most appropriate anyone could ever come up with, would *have* to be used again on this morning without fail and without excuse, just as in 1974.

With no other option available, Val and I had used our wait time the day before figuring out the guitar chords and memorizing the words, so it was now showtime. Without starting the generator, we snuck out the side door and turned on the "porch" light so we could see to set out our chairs. The three sleeping bags were arranged just behind Minnie Winnie so the light would illuminate us but not them, and after we got settled, I called out, "Gooood morning, Sandwalkers!"

That brought a couple muffled groans and some stirring, so we knew they were rising from the depths, and I began a few strums very unlike Credence Clearwater's pounding intro, as we began to sing out into the darkness. More muffled groaning ensued, but by the chorus they were fully awake, sort of sitting up in the shadows. (You'll notice no lyrics as explanation here, as sadly, it turns out copyright holders are slow to give permission, but quick to sue.)

We gave 'em a couple more bars and then, after it was apparent they were actually moving around a little, we bowed to a round of applause and went back inside to start the generator and get some coffee going.

That particular song carries magic with it on a trip like this, I tell you, because the Second Edition came clumping into the motor home in as good of spirits as we'd had forty-three years ago. In spite of—or perhaps because of—all the pain and soreness and misery accompanying these kinds of extreme outings, there is something about that song that just makes you grin, albeit painfully. It was deeply satisfying to pass that on to the next generation.

After another fine breakfast Val joined me in doctoring duties, which you would think would be fairly easy as both of us had been EMT attendants on Austin's Volunteer Ambulance Service for ten years, but which in fact was not, mainly because doctoring your own family is a lot harder than treating tourists. While I was tending Withanee's new and upcoming blisters I had a flashback to when I was a child draped over my father's knee after some perceived wrongdoing. He'd pulled off his leather belt and folded it in half, telling me before he used it as a future deterrent that this was going to hurt him a lot more than it was going to hurt me. That most certainly, decidedly, unmistakably was the biggest whopper I'd ever heard, right up until I became a father myself and found I couldn't stick a pin into a blister on my daughter's foot without passing out. I think Val finally did it, or maybe Josh, possibly even Shawn; I was too woozy to notice.

The next thing I knew the Second Edition was all geared up and out the door posing with their trademark fingers numbering the day, in this case Big Number Four. It was just starting to get light when they started down the wash to the highway, noticeably struggling to find comfortable strides. I didn't think they ever would but who knows? Then up from the trio came pleasingly clear strains of CCR's "Lookin' for a reason to stay," which brought smiles all around, again.

Val and I had our own canyon to contend with today. Highway 190 was set in straight stretches for the next 14 miles or so, but then it went snaking down into Panamint Valley in a most horrid way: 5 or 6 miles of very narrow, winding pavement lined on one side with guardrails perhaps a foot off the travel lane and fenced on the other by a vertical rocky cliff. I wasn't crazy about driving down the thing with either a motor home or the 4Runner, which had literally blown it on the last downhill it ran.

Day 4 smiles, brought to you by the Support Party and Creedence Clearwater.

Because the road was so treacherously narrow, there was no room to safely walk that portion, which was why the Sandwalkers were obliged to climb down a parallel canyon to the south. There didn't appear to be a safe way to drive down either, but I would certainly not trade the highways' descent for the one the Second Edition had coming up, thank you very much.

Before starting up the 4Runner, I checked the engine and surrounding area for the umpteenth time. I saw nothing at all out of the ordinary. I gingerly turned the key, and it started right up and purred like a kitten with no hint of distress. I still found that perplexing, and I wasn't looking forward to the steep downhill into Panamint Valley because it mimicked the grade coming off Mt. Whitney, which could easily cause another even more exciting mishap. However, there was nothing for it except to go and find out, so away we went.

Val followed in the Subaru, and we passed the walkers 2 or 3 miles up the road, honking and exchanging waves. At least the roadway here was somewhat level and looked not too gravelly. Of course the only way to know for sure was grip it with your own feet. Not me, not on this trip, thanks anyway.

It didn't take nearly long enough for the highway to get to the downhill part where I slowed way down and took a few deep breaths before dropping into third gear. This was where, as they say, the rubber met the road in the most telling way possible. The grade gradually steepened to the point where I found myself riding the brakes rather than trust engine compression to help check my speed. The, um, *last* time I tried that.... But I eventually had to take my foot off the brake pedal, thanking God I'd had new brakes installed just before we left on this trip, and was therefore at least ready to slam on the pedal at the first hint of tailpipe smoke or engine whining, but unlike what I was expecting the engine slowed the 4Runner nicely, without exploding.

Whew. If I didn't know better, I'd think I was a pessimist. Not that it wouldn't be justified in this case.

Still, the road was narrow and wound sharply about in a haphazard manner with all these restrictions in the way of cliffs and guardrails, so it was disconcerting to meet oncoming tour buses and motor homes that were obviously expecting to have their half of the highway all to themselves. Which only served to remind me that I'd have to bring our own motor home down there next. I had to admit that that did in fact trigger pessimistic thoughts.

Still, the fact that Val and I made it all the way to the bottom in two intact and separate pieces was very encouraging, both of us turning to the right into Darwin Wash just before the highway straightened out into Panamint Valley proper. Our plan was to set up camp in Darwin Wash a half-mile up the canyon, but that got revised by a sign that generally prohibited camping beyond the wash itself.

Well we'd have to fudge a bit because we lived in the desert and weren't about to camp in the wash itself, as flash floods are not just a figment of a pessimist's imagination. Some rules raise idiocy to a new and frightening level. I parked the 4Runner beyond where I was supposed to, locked it up, and hopped in the Subaru with Val. Nice guy that I am I offered to use my driving skills to pilot the Subaru back up that horrible road and Val said, "What horrible road?"

Alrighty then.

So back we went, Val humming along like she hadn't noticed what, exactly, this road demanded in the way of anxiety. I looked out the side window with feigned nonchalance, hoping she wouldn't realize where she was and panic. In essence I had to hang onto sanity for the both of us, but that's what good husbands do.

And thankfully, it worked. We arrived back at the motor home none the worse for wear, although we didn't visibly pass our walkers on the way. That, we understood, was because they were taking whatever shortcuts across the desert that presented themselves, and more power to them. They were able to find those shortcuts because of the huge technology gulf between 1974 and 2017. The digital mapping stuff they had now could show them practical ways to shorten the trip *while they were walking*, in addition to finding useful things like the secret oasis of the Mojave Desert, Jake's Saloon.

What an age we live in.

A few miles before we returned to the pulse-pounding downhill slalom we pulled off on a side road to set up the lunch wagon for our walkers. In addition to getting a closer start to the canyon than we had back then, they decided to follow the highway a couple miles farther with the idea of getting a better angle to cut across to the canyon's entrance. I thought that was a great adjustment, as in '74 we'd found the walking became difficult much sooner than we'd expected once we'd crossed beyond the hills visible from the highway.

When our Sandwalkers arrived they looked like they'd strayed into a cattle stampede, disheveled and dusty and really, really tired.

Next up? Nothing but The Canyon.

DRY WATERFALLS AREN'T THE ONLY OXYMORONS HERE

— *Withanee* —

In the Minnie sat the five of us, four idiots and my angel of a mother, who was busily cooking and cleaning and re-upping anything we needed, or might need, or could ever want. I took the opportunity to take my bandage off and ice my bum knee while my parents cooked my all-time favorite: fried egg sandwiches, Swiss cheese, extra mayo. This meal was a staple of my childhood, a specialty of my dad's, and we often survived on it as my mom worked long hours and we had to fend for ourselves on occasion. The other reason was that it required very few ingredients that we didn't normally have on hand.

I grew up in Austin, the dead center of Nevada, where grocery stores and outlet malls were a luxury we only saw in the movies. We drove a minimum 112 miles (one way) to Fallon for groceries, often extending that to 172 miles (also one way) to Reno, where Costco and the Meadowood Mall lived (*oooh, ahhh*). One could survive quite some time on bulk frozen Costco food, if the long-term planning and freezer size were just right.

Not to say we had nothing. The Schwan's man came from time to time to get us by, plus there was a gas station or two if we were in extreme need. And if we were, I never really knew it. Looking back now, it is clear that we traded all semblance of convenience for wide open space, adventure, the freedom to explore, play, and feel safe as a kid—and for the parent raising one.

I'd say we came out ahead.

There were somewhere around 150 residents of Austin and all the out-lying ranches back then, and I attended the smallest high school in the state of Nevada with about eighteen other kids. We had a lot of pride, though, and our sports program was surprisingly good, although we didn't have enough kids to have many subs or even scrape together an eight-man football team, which was fine by me. I never liked sitting on the bench anyway.

Time often turns your memories rosy, or at least it does for mine, and I will always have a soft spot in my heart for Austin and all the memories I made with my family there. Of course, I hated it in my teenage years, and I felt a rebellion bubbling up in my gut in my last year or so, exhausted with the small-town politics and yearning to blend into a crowd. I jetted out of there no sooner than I had turned my graduation tassel over, and I got my chance to brave the crowds at the University of Nevada, Reno. Turns out, city life never was fully what I built it up to be, although it was exactly what I needed at the time.

What's funny is, the same reasons I left in such a hurry are all the same reasons I go back now. I just love God's sense of humor.

Anyway, I wish I could say all that life reflection stuff went through my brain as I happily inhaled my sandwich on the side of Highway 190 that day, but all I could think was how delicious it was. In fact, I was thinking, "Geez. I wouldn't mind another." My cohorts joined me, and we all had a second round of fried egg sandwiches. I probably could have tackled a third, but they seemed to be done and I didn't want to make a pig of myself.

I can't help but wonder if my parents didn't plan my favorite lunch on Canyon Day on purpose, likened to a death row inmate and their last meal. They didn't say anything to that effect, but I did notice that both Mom and Dad hugged me a little tighter as we went to leave, almost like they weren't entirely confident they'd ever see me again.

We set off, armed with GPS mapping, full bellies, and Dad's instructions from forty-three years ago. We knew this could get tricky, because there were two canyons and we needed to get into the one farthest north. Sounds simple enough, but on the ground it is really hard to tell these things. I think we all sort of expected to walk maybe 20 or 30 minutes before being funneled into our canyon, but apparently it was much farther than my pea brain comprehended and took much longer than any of us expected. Mark my words, though, such is always, always the case.

Some vague number of miles later, we stumbled upon a curious clearing. Where the rest of the ground was somewhat brushy, this was suspiciously, erm, *not*. The cleared portion was circular in shape, large, and outlined in rocks. Outside of that circle was a post, maybe three inches in diameter and sticking out of the ground about four feet. At the base of the post was metal caging, filled with rocks. There were also piles of rocks filled with brush and smaller rocks in the area. I need to probably reiterate here that we were in total desolation, I mean the absolute *north-forty*, so the logic here was nil. We paused to poke around a little bit, something Sandwalkers are wont to do, with the most cerebral of us, Josh (of course), trying a couple of explanations on for size. Could be Native Americans, he reasoned. Maybe a burial ground. In my crisp and totally uninjured hindsight, I realize here that the *least cerebral* of us just walked straight on through it. I clambered my way straight through the large, rock-lined clearing, up over the piles, all of it. I can't even be sure I didn't sit on that post. So, if indeed it was a burial ground or something of that nature, I feel pretty bad about that. Among so many other little delights, pain really does make a person rude. Of course, it could have been an alien rock crop circle, in which case I would have certainly welcomed the ride out of that miserable desert, and I don't regret it one bit.

Not having come up with any certifiable explanation but exhausting our already feeble minds, we limped on. Shortly thereafter, we heard a rumbling sound in the distance.

"This is my chance," I thought. "If it's aliens, they are my ticket out of here!"

No such luck, but we did see a couple of military cargo transport jets zooming overhead, suspiciously low to the ground and shake-your-teeth loud.

Curiouser and curiouser.

By then it was hot and very desert-y out there, and my navigators' voices kind of drifted in and out of my brain as they were having some sort of musings about our location. I couldn't bring their voices into focus, but I knew they were discussing our position as being headed toward the very thing my dad warned us to avoid: the wrong canyon. Luckily they worked that one out, and we repositioned our little selves to continue in a more northerly manner, instead of entering the canyon we were closest to. Thanks, Dad.

I felt like those 4 miles from the Minnie Winnie and egg sandwiches took days to walk, but eventually we found ourselves at the mouth of the beast. We stopped to rest at my request, and I had myself a snack and a long stare at that shiny thing on my finger. I took a little video of it sparkling up at me, thinking to myself that if I die in here at least my skeleton will be sporting some bling. Too shortly thereafter, Josh had us up and moving again with all the encouragement of someone who wasn't on the precipice of the gates of hell.

The first 100 feet or so weren't too bad and, actually, it was even a little sandy. Ahhhh. Good walking, that sand. That happy little thought lasted almost all of five minutes, and soon we were traversing down sharp, steep boulders. As I sit here today, totally healed up and healthy, I don't honestly know if I could stand up and go scamper down the rock ledges we faced in that canyon. How we did it in the pathetic condition we were in I can't say, except to quote an excerpt from my dad's journey so many years before me: "None of us had any intention at all of going anywhere but forward."

Well that's a poetic way of putting it. Another way, and perhaps more descriptive of my own personal experience, was that there was no way in *helllll* I was bushwhacking back that 4 miles to the highway. That really left me no other choice than to wearily trudge along, picking my way from boulder to boulder. I winced in pain every time I had to step up onto a rock that was bigger than my car on a knee that may well have been an elbow, for all the good it did me. Years later, I can still feel ghosts of that pain.

It didn't take long for us to come to the first appetizer that the canyon would serve up—dry falls. I hadn't ever really heard that term before reading about my dad's walk, and even then the true definition didn't appropriately permeate my brain. It wasn't until that very moment that I understood what Dad meant. Dry *waterfalls*. Waterfalls, without the, well, water. Heck of an oxymoron, eh? Sheer vertical drops of rocks that no human had any business being near, and yet here we were. We paused, and then my brand-spanking-new fiancé went to work lowering himself down, pack and all, light as a feather.

Show off.

He then used his walking stick to point to which rock was stable enough for me to step on and slowly make my way down to him. Josh remained behind me in case he could catch me by my pigtails if I were to do what we were all thinking I'd do. Though no one voiced it, we were all of the same mind. If one of us were to get hurt in that canyon, we knew

The most friendly of the dry falls.

there was a very slim chance of getting them help. There was no cell service, no radio communication with our support party, zilch. Carrying someone back up the canyon would be impossible, and going down to the bottom wasn't a viable option either, as the going would be even slower than it already was. The sidewalls were certainly impossible to climb out of, so, that was pretty much that. It was no longer a fun adventure I could quit at any time; this was the moment that the seriousness and validity of The Walk changed for me.

I was dangerously close to a temper tantrum.

What started as an appetizer quickly became the main course, and there were at least five more of those dry falls, all a minimum of 20 feet in height and varying degrees of ridiculousness. Josh later told me that his stomach dropped every time he watched me fumble my way down, terrified I would fall to my death. Funny, I felt the same way.

Those dry falls by themselves would have been enough, I think, to classify us as *stark-raving-crazy-nuts,* and that canyon as the worst thing, *ever.* What's sad is, I don't even know if I can say that the dry falls were the worst part. They were up there, for sure, but in between them were twists, turns, huge boulders that we had to climb up and then slide down, and the most jagged and painful rocks a foot could ever step on. Did I mention spider webs the size of a small child that harbored, oh yea, tarantulas?

So. Much. Fun.

One telltale sign of the horrible terrain we were on was in the form of broken burro hooves scattered amongst the boulders. Boy, do I get it now. This was evidence that burros had tried to make their way down that canyon, but it totally annihilated their hooves, leaving splinters and pieces and bones behind. Let me tell you, I understood that so completely. Only jackasses attempted that canyon.

Many hours later, the walls of the canyon began to widen out. I thought for sure we had done it— declare us survivors of the Canyon of Horrors. When we looked, we all noticed that the rock color had changed to a dramatic green. I kept mumbling, "The Emerald City, Dorothy!" It was strange, and Shawn even picked up a couple pieces of that weird green rock, one to give to Dad and one to take for ourselves. I'd say that was a fair trade, my soul for a piece of stupid green rock.

The widening walls and the "Emerald City" were misnomers though, as we still had quite a ways to go. I kept trying to get Dad on the radio dangling from the front strap of my pack, but my pleas were met with a ghostly silence on the other end.

Finally, just as the sun had set and the dark was threatening to close in on us, we heard a loud crackle on the radio.

"With, are you there?"

I stopped dead in my tracks. I fumbled with the radio until I could whimper back to my dad.

My God. We were almost out of that dreaded canyon, and in the absolute nick of time. I dug my headlamp out of my pack, and we kept moving, now able to see the headlights of the Toyota 4Runner in the distance. Mom wandered out to meet us, without a headlamp or a flashlight, and I got a little worried about her in the dark. All's well that ends OK, though, and next thing I knew we were stumbling up to them in the dark, safely out of that. Damned. Canyon.

Dad was as happy to see us as we were him, and as it turns out, they were just leaving to go back to camp when he thought he would radio me one last time. Worried sick, he threw up a hail Mary in the dark. I guess I can understand. To be fair, he was the reason we were out there in the first place, and only he and three other Original Sandwalkers could possibly understand the nightmare we had just been through.

We got to the high fives waiting from our support party 10 minutes after 7 p.m., and it was the first time I saw Shawn keel over on the entire walk. I could tell my parents had been worried, but they also were looking a bit sheepishly at me, and my spidey senses knew something was up. I probably should have noticed that there was nary a Minnie Winnie in sight.

Dad took a deep breath, "Well, uh, you've still got just a *little* farther to go. That is, unless you want us to drive you down to the camp spot and then drive you back here tomorrow morning."

"WHAT?!"

How could that be? We weren't done with the day yet, we still had two more stinking miles to go. I started to panic when both Josh and Shawn looked at me and said, "But With, there's beer. Flat terrain . . . and there's beer."

Dad handed us some IPAs and away we went. Mom even joined us for a short time, though she was so speedy that none of us could hobble fast enough to keep up with her—not without spilling our beers, at least. She eventually jumped in the Toyota when Dad came back up to replenish the brew, and they headed off to camp to fix dinner.

Two more miles and voila! I do think that "voila" was the beer. In my infinite post-Walk-and-Canyon-pocalypse wisdom, I know this one truth: beer is absolute proof that God really loves us and wants us to be happy. Shameless plug here for Sierra Nevada Brewery, thank you for your service.

We ended that wretched 20-mile day with hotdogs, beans, more beer, and Dad reading us the customary story for the next day. I said a prayer as I drifted off to a painful sleep, thankful for our survival and vowing never to walk in *any* canyon again for the rest of my life.

Amen.

CANYON OF LOST SOLES

—Jim—

For lunch Withy had requested one of my staples from when she was growing up: fried egg sandwiches topped with melted Swiss cheese, so that's what they got. I tried hard not to connect the dots to condemned prisoner's "last meals," which, I found out later, Withy also considered, but I wasn't able to entirely convince myself, and when they limped away toward the hills Val and I held each other. One reason was that Val wanted to go with them, just to the top of those hills a mile or so away, just to make sure they'd get the right start, you see. I dissuaded her by pointing out we still had lots to do before setting up camp—taking Minnie Winnie on into Panamint Springs for replenishment for one thing and finding a level campsite amongst the rocks lining the wash for another, a site that wasn't too flagrantly breaking the rules. She finally agreed, but it wasn't easy for her, and we silently watched until the Sandwalkers Second Edition disappeared beyond the crest of the distant hills.

As they headed for their canyon we headed for ours, Minnie balking a little by way of the engine dying once while turning around. Didn't blame her in the least. I wasn't happy to be looking forward to it either.

A couple miles later we began the fairly straight downhill part, the canyon proper not beginning until just beyond the viewing area known as Father Crowley Overlook. What it overlooked was a deep rock-walled canyon to the north of the highway where a portion of the *Star Wars* saga was filmed. I'd never stopped there, mainly because I'd seen too much of these canyons already. I almost did stop this time though, but if I had, I was fully aware that I'd have a tough time starting up again. No, best not to hesitate at the edge of the pool, best just to jump on in as had been my habit for the last seventy years or so, and I was able to resist a strong urge to overturn it on this one. I did find it necessary to get a white-knuckled grip on the steering wheel though, and to turn my baseball cap backward in the manner of Clint Eastwood's sidekick on *Every Which Way but Loose* which was the manner I intended to hang on.

I'd already driven this road twice, once coming up in the Minnie Winnie last week and once going down in the 4Runner today, and having that experience I, unlike Val, was not about to put on a happy face. I tried mightily not to hold my breath with only marginal success, the longest being when we passed an oncoming motor home on a switchback that funneled us between two vertical rock faces. It was clear to both he and I that we weren't going to fit, and I'm sure he was as surprised as I was when we inched "safely" past at maybe a quarter-of-a-mile per hour. After that the rest of it was, as they say, a piece of cake, and I was able to breathe now and then all the way to the bottom.

We turned into Darwin Wash but were unable to find a rock-free level area anywhere within a reasonable distance of the "day use only" sign, so we decided we'd have to stay in the wash itself for the night. Well, odds were there wouldn't be a flash flood around here tonight, or in the next year for that matter, so we bucked up and leveled a place as near the edge as we could find. Still, if one lives in the desert one gets uneasy camping in a dry wash, and I certainly did. Back in 1974 there were no restrictions on these open spaces; it wasn't until President Clinton expanded Death Valley by a million acres and changed its designation from a national monument to a national park that things got all gummed up in bureaucracy. Sadly, it is doubtful it will ever become ungummed.

After we got our campsite figured out Val and I took Minnie into Panamint Springs to refuel and replenish. There isn't a whole lot there, but the gas station/mini-mart also rents out camping spaces across the highway, and we went ahead and reserved one for tomorrow night, not for camping but because they had hookups we could use and indoor shower rooms for guests. We had a shower available in the motor home and it got a lot of use, but as anybody who's used one can tell you motor home showers are a bit cramped, and you begin to long for an area big enough that you can turn around in without bumping into walls. We thought to bring the Sandwalkers back to Panamint Springs from wherever we made camp tomorrow night for a turnaround shower and perhaps a meal at the restaurant there. It would be an option anyway, depending on whether or not the walkers were up to it.

With that Val and I returned to the campsite and parked Minnie as close into the bank as we could, as if that would do any good. Then we arranged the Subaru just upstream of it and decided to explore Darwin Wash in the 4Runner.

The Original Sandwalkers had camped perhaps 300 yards upstream of where we were, to the south of the dirt road in a wide turnout. Surprisingly enough we had never gone on up the wash from there, and the only time I saw that campsite in the daylight was the morning we awoke after getting in after dark the night before. The reason I found that surprising was that as we ate breakfast that long-ago morning I was faced upstream, and I assumed we had walked into camp from the canyon I could see from where I was sitting. All these years later that didn't look right, and as Val and I started up the wash it was obvious that wasn't the canyon we'd walked out of because it dead-ended about a block into it. So I told Val we must have come out of the canyon mouth just above it, but when we looked at that one it was a dead end also. Canyon after canyon spilled into Darwin Wash as we climbed, and still, they were all superficial, not particularly going anywhere, and certainly not several miles into the backcountry.

When we finally came to the one that fit the criteria, I was utterly astonished; we were almost 2 miles above our campsite. Of course we'd walked a good 2 hours into darkness back then, but when we finally came into our camp I had assumed we'd just then spilled out of the side canyon into our campsite in Darwin Wash.

Not so. Anyone who studies the map would see that easily, so how in the world had I missed it? And more to the immediate point, how was I going to explain it to the Second Edition now fighting their way down that torturous expanse of misery at that very moment? Assuming, that is, that they'd survived thus far. It was starting to get late, and as I studied what I could see of the canyon floor through my binoculars, nothing was moving except for the lengthening shadows, reminding us that the sun was going down.

I finally turned to Val, who was starting to get antsy and about ready to head up the canyon on foot, and suggested we go back to the motor home. I thought we should get the spotlight and fill the ice chest with water and beer and come back to wait for them. She agreed that was probably the best we could do, but suggested she wait for them just in case while I ran the errand. Not a bad idea, if I left her with a radio and flashlight, but I was torn about splitting up yet again. So I tried one more call on the radio.

"Hey Withy, can you hear me?'

Silence...and then crackle, crackle.

"Dad! Hey! I can see the Yoda, I can see the Yoda!"

And there, just coming into sight around some rocks, a flash of white, no, two, no, three! They made it! At least within a half-mile or so. There was still a considerable rocky walk to be made to get over to where we were, but I don't know if I've ever been as happy and relieved and just downright joyful as I was at that moment. And Val too. We hugged and Val took off, leaping over rocks to get up there and join them. I hollered at her out of habit, but as usual it didn't take and I really didn't mind anyway.

As they made their way across they were hollering things like, "OGs rule! You came through this in the dark? OGs rule!"

They were very vocal in their astonishment of us OGs, the OG referring of course to the "Original Sandwalkers," not "Old Guys"' (I think). Either way, it was a nice confirmation that the canyon really was a special tunnel of horrors and not something I'd added to in my mind over the intervening years.

However, if ever I'd been blessed with a well-behaved mind I would have right then taken the 4Runner (which you might have noticed was nicknamed "Yoda" by the way) down to the motor home and loaded up. I could have returned with some ice and cold beer before they reached Darwin Wash Road. But I didn't. I watched the sun go down as the Second Edition struggled across the rocky expanse, Val happily keeping them in tow, finally reaching the roadway just as dark settled in. They were confused as to where the motor home was.

"Well, um," I stammered, "Um, the campsite is still a little bit down the road you see. I thought the canyon um, you know, um, came out down there and, um, it didn't."

Val jumped in and explained it too, perhaps better than I had, with the result that it visibly deflated our charges.

"You mean," my daughter asked incredulously, "we have to walk some more? Now?"

Well, yes.

She deflated even more, resembling a towed balloon slowly sagging out of Macy's Thanksgiving Day Parade.

Josh and Shawn both righted the ship as best they could, bless them, by pointing out that from here on down they wouldn't be threading their way around boulders and rockfalls, they'd be walking a presentable dirt road. I nodded and told them I'd be back in a heartbeat with some frosty IPAs.

Val walked with them while I made the round trip as quickly as I could without dusting everybody into oblivion, and when I returned we lowered the tailgate. They finally got to sit down and enjoy something, which hadn't happened since we left them after lunch, and you could sense the relaxation flowing, although it was flowing into the dark of night.

We didn't try to hurry them along at all, and of their own accord they unfolded themselves after about 20 minutes and thanked us, of all things. Stuff like that is heartening.

I took Val back to the motor home where she cooked up beans and franks while I rearranged the 4Runner. By the time dinner was ready we could hear them outside, the timing flawless. After dinner they cleaned up, went out and set up their campsite, and then they returned for a cold one, some doctoring, and our nightly reading of tomorrow's chapter.

I never did get used to reading my own story out loud, but if these three wanted to hear it I felt obliged to provide it. I so easily remembered how terribly difficult that walk was, and how things that seemed trivial and pointless got magnified when you actually just needed to take your mind off yourself for a moment.

Well they came to the right place; I've got enough pointless trivia to obscure even myself, let alone anybody who listens.

And more power to us Sandwalkers, especially those of us who conquered the Canyon. I do believe the Canyon was the place where the sole of my new and expensive hiking boot started to separate, finally breaking loose midway across Death Valley. And the Second Edition also shared with me the appalling discovery of wild burro's broken hooves in that canyon, which my bunch never noticed.

Accordingly, it wouldn't be far-fetched at all to call it the "Canyon of Lost Soles."

UNFORESEEN DANGERS—ROAD SIGNS AND BLOW DRYERS

— *Withanee* —

Day five dawned, but the Sandwalkers did not. We had somewhat planned this sleep-in as a reward for surviving the day before, and by golly, I think we earned it. Eventually, I poked my pounding head out from the depths of my sleeping bag, groaned, and burrowed back in. Josh was already up and in search of coffee, but Shawn was peacefully snoozing away. I stuck my hand high in the air and checked my ring to make sure it was still there. It was, looking as clean and gleaming as it had when Shawn had popped it out on Mt. Whitney. It didn't even look like it had gone with me yesterday: not a speck of dirt, tears, or blood on it. Several times throughout the week, Shawn and my dad had tried to talk me out of wearing it during the rest of The Walk. Shawn had purchased it a couple of sizes too large, and they were both afraid it would slip off and be lost forever. I understood their point—I really shouldn't be trusted with something that expensive, but their worries turned out to be irrelevant. My fingers were so fat and swollen that we couldn't have gotten that thing off with a Costco-size tub of Crisco, let alone it slip off on its own accord. Wouldn't have mattered anyway. I had waited three, nay thirty, years for that ring, and you'd have to all but kill me to make me part with it.

Josh caught me, and I imagine it must have looked pretty funny with just my hand in the air, poking out of my nest of a sleeping bag with no other signs of life. His hunt for coffee had turned up empty. Mom and Dad were having problems with the generator this morning. They got it running eventually, and I finally sat up in my bag. Shawn was alive too, and soon enough we were having our coffee and packing up the day's gear.

Spirits were high, which must have had something to do with the idea that we were past the hard part. Ha.

We posed for our morning's photo, looking quite proud of ourselves:

Bring on the day, maybe.

This day would bring, what else? More walking. The days were getting hotter as we made our way to Death Valley, and this morning was particularly still, something Dad warned me years before that usually meant the day would be a scorcher. As usual, he was right.

We said goodbye to our support party and slithered back out onto the highway toward Panamint Springs. Shawn was in a particularly good mood and kept stealing glances back at Dad, who was sitting in his lawn chair sipping coffee and looking out over the rugged and sprawling landscape. Something about that image was incredibly beautiful; maybe it was the backdrop, but more likely it was the look on my sweet dad's face. There was a peaceful, almost reverent feeling to it and I wasn't the only one who noticed. Shawn was *fixated* and kept stealing glances backward.

"Oh man. There really isn't anything better. I wish I was up there right now, having coffee with him and relaxing. I just love mornings like that, like at work when I get to drink coffee and watch the sunrise. . . ."

SMACK.

Josh, being in the lead, spun around to see what the noise was. I had been walking right behind Shawn and had to put on the brakes so hard it brought searing pain to my knee and tears to my eyes. A different kind of tears came when I realized what had happened: in all of his daydreaming and looking backward, my future husband had walked face-first into a highway signpost. The way his body seemed to wrap around the pole and remain that way, probably only for a split second but to us it was like time had frozen, he looked *exactly* like a cartoon character. For the second time that week, he had all of us in a howling, bent-over fit of laughter. I love the sound of my brother's laugh, so even when I would start winding down, Josh's howls would get me going again. I vividly remember him actually sticking out his arm and pointing at Shawn with one hand, holding his stomach with the other. Later that afternoon Dad would ask us what all the commotion was, as our laughter was so loud it drifted up the canyon to his cozy little lawn chair. Boy, did we have fun telling him.

We followed the highway down to Panamint Springs, where Josh and Shawn found a two-track road that led us off of that uncomfortable highway walking a little sooner than we had planned. We made our way onto the dry lake bed of Panamint Valley, and it was definitely hot, though nowhere near as hot as it had been when Dad had crossed it in '74. We were all grateful for that, at least, though add in sunburnt lips to my ever-growing list of pleasantries.

Walking across the dry lake bed wasn't the best, but it wasn't the worst either. The cracked ground felt better on my knee than some of the other terrain we had encountered up to this point, so there was that. The kicker was definitely the heat, and the fact that the lake bed seemed to stretch out with no end in sight. The hours spent on that bed are simply a blur of heat waves and chapped lips, and Shawn occasionally throwing up a small rock and hitting it with his stick. Our support party found us at some point or another, set up folding chairs for us, and supplied ice packs, handfuls of Advil, lunch, and cold drinks. Man, do I love them.

After lunch, our course took a painful turn for me. The road after the lake bed was rocky, and for some reason the bottoms of my feet chose that

All aboard the train to Desolation Station.

moment to start their protest and began cramping and having spasms. At first I thought I was just dehydrated, but I ruled that out after having consumed enough water to flood the valley, to no relief.

There is a lesson here. I spent months trying to decide what kind of shoes would be most appropriate for this walk because I knew that choice would *really* matter. Happy feet are crucial. I also knew that I needed to break them in before the trek, because my dad had made the horrible mistake of not breaking his in so many years before me. I searched and searched for shoes, and I even ended up taking one pair back to REI after about a week of wear when they just didn't feel perfect. I finally ended up driving an hour from my house to Tahoe City to a shop with a truly knowledgeable gal who had hiked Mt. Whitney more than once. I didn't want to get stiff hiking boots, but I also couldn't wear flimsy running shoes, so I went in search of advice. I spent over an hour talking about my options with her when finally we settled on a shoe that was tennis in nature but she swore would work great for both ends of my trip, mountain and desert. I slipped them on and had my "a-ha" moment. They felt like a Tempur-Pedic mattress for my feet. I sighed and bounced my way around the store, feeling like I had giant marshmallow puffs on my feet and grinning like an idiot at everyone in my path. Sold.

I paid a pretty penny for those marshmallows, more than $150, and I had the highest hopes in the world for them. I called my dad immediately after my big purchase, and he was excited for me but warned me to break them in ASAP. I did, kind of, but since they were so soft and cushy I wasn't too worried about it. I felt sure I had made the best decision and would not regret it.

Fast forward to Josh, Shawn, and I sitting on a very rocky two-track road on the second half of day five, all staring at my pretty pink and *expensive* marshmallow shoes while I try to tamper a brewing meltdown. As it turns out, the fact that the bottoms of my shoes were so squishy was a negative thing. It allowed the soles to bend around rocks, making my feet feel light as a feather *but* eventually wore them to the condition they were in. This newest monkey wrench in my physical condition was a bad one, and I now limped not only because of my knee but also both of my cramped feet. I put as much weight as I could on my trekking poles and crutched along, but it was very slow and painful going. We funneled out onto Wildrose Road, where we had planned to forge on for 3 or 4 more miles, but I just couldn't do it. I was grumpy and in pain and I pleaded my case to my fellow Sandwalkers. We met with our support party and decided to camp, effectively completing one of our shortest mileage days that week just shy of 17 miles. My bad.

After The Walk, I never wore those shoes again. It almost made me stop eating marshmallows. Almost.

I think everyone could sense my mood, and soon my group had decided that we would load up in Josh's Subaru and Mom and Dad would drive us back to Panamint Springs, where there were camp spots for rent with showers and a restaurant. *Showers!* Beer. Food. Suddenly my feet were starting to relax from their balled-up fists of fury.

The drive back to Panamint Springs was dizzying to say the least. It was somewhere to the tune of forty minutes back over the same ground we had covered that day. I hadn't done anything but walk and drink beer for the last five days, and the speed at which everything was flying by was making me sick. I hung my head and squeezed my eyes shut until we pulled into the camp space that my parents had rented for us, just so that we could all have access to the showers.

And ooooh did I shower. Mom and I split away from the boys, and I limped to the women's showers wearing my flippy flops. I stood under piping hot water for as long as I possibly could. It. Was. Glorious. Every muscle in my body was thankful for that shower, and my mood had improved significantly by the time I got out. The walls were somewhat thin, and I could hear the guy's voices mumbling on the other side as Mom and I chatted and I brushed out my dripping hair. I guess this is where I will admit something a little embarrassing, for the sake of posterity and the fact that I still haven't lived it down. Thing is, I have really wild hair, OK? It is super curly, frizzy, hard to manage, and obnoxious in a way that everyone asks me where the hell it came from when they see it in its natural state. If I dare let it dry without the help of tools, such as a blow dryer or straightener, I look very much like a tumbleweed in a windstorm. So, as I was talking to mom, I got a little fixated on an electrical outlet I saw hiding under the sink and saw an opportunity. I guess I lost sight that I was in a campground shower for goodness sake, not the Four Seasons. I excitedly dug through my backpack and whipped out my trusty old blow dryer, plugging it in and firing it up while Mom stared at me in wonderment. It took all of 30 seconds for the circuit breaker to blow and power to the entire campground to go out.

I stared in horror at my mom.

"Oh boy, was that my fault?!"

Mom started throwing her shower stuff in her bag and making moves to run. From the other side of the wall I could hear the unmistakable sound of my brother and fiancé roaring with laughter. Great.

Mom and I scampered out of the bathroom and back to the Subaru. As the guys rounded the corner, I knew by their faces that the jig was up.

"Tell me you didn't just knock out the power to the entire campground with a blow dryer?!" Shawn said incredulously.

Silence.

"With, why do you even have that thing with you?!" Josh asked.

Silence.

I don't know this to be certain, but in my mind I can still feel everyone in that campground's eyes on me and my blow dryer. I dumped the evidence in the back of the Subaru, and we all made our way across the street to the restaurant/bar. Another fun little tidbit here that possibly got overshadowed by my big blunder was the fact that Josh, Shawn, and I all came out of the showers with the exact same shirt on. We had run a Spartan race together the year prior, and somehow we had picked that night to wear the t-shirt that we had been awarded for having completed the race. It was not preplanned whatsoever, but it sure was funny. Much funnier than the, er, other thing.

Dinner that night was a blast, and as we sipped our beers and my hair grew bigger and fuzzier, we were all treated to the exact medicine my aching body needed: laughter and a slight buzz.

A ROUND TRIP TO PANAMINT SPRINGS

—Jim—

As everybody knows, all good things eventually come to an end. And so it was that our morning alarm clock mostly failed. I say "mostly" because the generator powering up was the usual signal for our charges to get ready for some coffee and breakfast and walking, and this morning our generator didn't power up at all. It did crank and crank and crank with enough noise to waken our sleepers just outside on the ground, but it wouldn't do what we relied on it to do: start up and make our coffee grounds drinkable since it was early in the morning, the time all Americans require drinkability with their caffeine.

Darn.

Val, ever the optimist, heated water in a pan on the propane stove while I got out the motor home rental instructions. I seemed to remember the nice folks who rented Minnie to us mentioned something about... well, something to do with all the accessories in case they didn't perform as advertised. By following the written directions, which is kind of a stretch for me, I did indeed find the culprit: a tripped circuit breaker in the generator compartment, and within a very few minutes we were back in business, with a stovetop pan of hot water to boot. Having seen my share of Western movies over the decades I was certain that hot water would come in handy for the morning doctorin' somehow, so I started with my daughter's knee. It seemed swollen more than it was yesterday so we iced it in hopes of getting the swelling down a little before wrapping it with an ace bandage. No use for the hot water there, but we did use some of it for cleaning around the blisters on her feet before applying moleskin.

We also used some on Josh's award-winning double blister, but we still had plenty of hot water if someone were to suffer, say, an outlaw bullet or arrow. The country we were traveling through certainly looked prime for that sort of thing.

Happily nothing like that came to pass, but our walkers were away a bit later than usual. That wasn't due to the generator as much as it was sleeping in; yesterday's exertions through the canyon had required a longer sleep-recovery period, just as it had us on the original walk. Curious how so many things on this walk seemed to correspond to the original walk. Funny and unnerving, when I thought ahead to things like Gary's attempt to ride a wild burro. Still gives me shivers.

I let all that stuff go as the Second Edition saddled up and posed for their customary finger-count picture of the fifth day of their walk. Then I lowered myself into a folding chair to watch as they hobbled away.

Throughout this whole project I was fully aware that Withanee was recreating my trek of 1974, but as I sat there watching them walk toward the rising sun I had an extremely strong sense of my daughter walking out of *my* past and into *her* future. I suppose that had been happening her whole life, but if so it had never been manifest on such a magnificent and singular scale. The closest I can come to describing the feeling is to compare it with the immensity you feel the first time you see the Grand Canyon. Dizzying, in a breathtaking manner that is surprisingly pleasing. Wow.

They dwindled and faded out of sight when they crossed the highway into the shadow of a mountain, and as I sat there nursing a steaming cup of coffee I was completely unaware that Shawn was, as I was told later, distracted by looking back at me comfortably sitting there, which resulted in him inadvertently wrapping himself at walking speed around a metal highway signpost a la Roger Rabbit in Toontown. I knew only something happened that caused laughter to echo throughout the canyon, and although the whole incident was invisible from where I was sitting I could distinctly pick out the guffaws of Withanee and Josh, quickly followed by Shawn's. It seemed like it went on for a long time.

After an enjoyable interlude in which Val and I just relaxed and joked around a bit we locked up Minnie and set out to find the next relay point with the 4Runner and the Subaru. Since we had no idea how far the walkers would go on this day, or even what route they might end up taking, we could only guess at where we ought to set up. It wasn't all guesswork of course because we knew their route was to head south toward Wildrose Canyon Road in order to cross the Panamint Mountains, but as the support party we did indeed want to stay in radio range on the walkie-talkies, just in case. So the first bit was pretty short; after fueling up at Panamint Springs we drove 2½ miles to Panamint Valley Road and turned south. We pulled over and left Yoda at a turnout about a mile south of the junction with Highway 190 near a rock and wood marker designating the boundary of Death Valley National Park.

That was new to me because the boundary to Death Valley Monument in 1974 was several miles to the southeast in Wildrose Canyon. You know, much, much closer to, um, Death Valley. Must be an optical illusion because I would have sworn Death Valley itself hadn't grown that much since then.

We returned to Darwin Wash, for the last time ever I hoped, and retrieved Minnie Winnie from the danger of drowning in a flash flood. After replenishing everything once more at Panamint Springs we drove back to the park boundary, finding some tourists posing for pictures in front of the Death Valley sign. They were taking turns being the photographer, and having seen that before I offered to help. They were grateful and handed me the cameras so they could all group around the sign. I took three or four, hoping at least one would come out in focus, and they asked what Sandwalkers were. I didn't remember until then that both Val and I were wearing the shirts Withanee had made for us, the ones with the words "Sandwalkers" along with "Mt. Whitney to Death Valley" printed on them, so I felt obligated to explain what we were doing. In the meantime Val had contacted our walkers with the radio so I was able to point to the distant hikers out there in the sagebrush and cactus waving back at us. The tourists had obviously been doing their homework and were in awe of anybody actually walking between those two points.

"Me too," I said, and I wasn't lying. I explained the whole thing as best I could and the tourists, who Val thought were Canadian, seemed kind of at a loss as to what to say. They stared in the general direction of our walkers, which was also the general direction of Mt. Whitney, and then turned and stared at the Panamint Mountains behind us, which was the general direction of Death Valley.

I have no idea if they regarded us as sterling examples of mankind's spirit of adventure or if they just thought we were some kind of extra-special stupid. Truth to tell I've never figured that one out myself.

There were smiles and waves when our Canadians left, and I found I'd really enjoyed their brief visit. We made some sort of connection that'll stay with me, and although it baffles me I'm grateful for it; it brings me closer to our Creator when I sense how much He values each and every one of us. The older I get the weaker the theory of evolution becomes until now it's downright wispy. If you've ever seen a heavy ground fog burned off by the morning sun, it's like that.

We relayed the 4Runner 6½ miles down to Minietta Road, a dirt track running east across Panamint Valley, and came back for Minnie. Our walkers were just coming down the alluvial fan toward Panamint Dry Lake. They told us via radio they were good to meet us for lunch somewhere to the south of the dry lake, so off we went, knowing we'd have to leave the motor home at the junction of Minietta Road.

Minietta Road was not motor-home friendly so we'd have to use the 4Runner as today's Taco Truck. That wasn't without misgivings, but the engine had performed flawlessly since it "blew up" on Whitney Portal Road and we decided to chance it. I was aware there was an old road running north-south above the lake bed as we'd walked it in '74, so I wasn't concerned about finding a place to meet the Second Edition. I suppose I should have been concerned, the desert having since been groomed into a national park so cleverly you'd never notice.

Sure enough, a mile or so down Minietta Road we came to an old crossroad that I hadn't seen on my trip, and the left side of the junction, toward the dry lake bed, sported a sign reading "No Motor Vehicles." Well, no big deal; that wasn't the road I was headed for so it wasn't my ox that'd been gored.

After another mile Minietta Road dead-ended into the road we *were* headed for and, off to the left again, stood a sign right smack in the middle of the road saying, "No Motor Vehicles."

My poor gored ox flopped lifelessly into the dust like the useless pest it was. Well who needs 'em anyway? However, we could neither raise our walkers on the radio nor see them anywhere out there, even with 10× binoculars, and that made me nervous. When us OGs walked this valley the temperature was a good ten or fifteen degrees higher, but this day was still hotter than blazes. There were enough heat ripples distorting the lake

101

Thank goodness for trekking poles.

bed that we wouldn't be able to see them at this distance anyway, and our walkers were probably just fine.

Still. . . .

To us the circumstances were such that we were willing to risk the consequences and I drove around the sign. The road was washed out in several places, requiring four-wheel drive. It was slow going, and we stopped often to scan the lake bed and try the radio. After an hour or so Withy came in loud and clear, telling us she could see Yoda far off to their left and that we were about even with them. She said they were finally off the lake bed and headed due south, so we turned Yoda around and went all the way back to the road where we'd seen the first "No Motor Vehicles" sign, this time keeping on the legal side.

We set out chairs and Val made lunch, putting the finishing touches on just as the Second Edition came limping in. Sandwiches and watermelon and Gatorade later they looked marginally better, but my heart still went out to them. They were clearly running on fumes—especially Withy—but their toughness and determination overruled it enough that they posed for an extraordinarily cheerful photo before heading out again.

After they faded from view on their way to Wildrose Canyon, Val and I packed up and drove back to Minnie Winnie on Minietta Road. I remember thinking that had a nice ring to it, but what had a nicer ring was the purring of the 4Runner engine after going through the paces it had labored through that day. Considering the Whitney Portal incident, it still seemed downright impossible.

From where we were it was necessary to leapfrog our three vehicles 6½ miles south to Wildrose Canyon Road, which then required another 6 miles traveling northeast to get to where we hoped to camp, a point about 6 total miles from where we lunched with our walkers. It was quite roundabout but our longer route was infinitely easier than their shorter one, clearly demonstrated by their depleted condition when they came dragging into the campsite. We were parked on a turnout just below an open swivel-pipe gate that was apparently kept closed at times. The gate hadn't been around in 1974 but then neither had the Second Edition Sandwalkers, so I guess it evened out.

As near as I could figure, the gate was about where the Death Valley Monument sign had been back then, which I confirmed by putting our old picture above the morning shot of the Second Edition.

The mountains in the background match perfectly, but the road we'd walked on to get to Wildrose Canyon no longer existed, which made for a very rocky trek since we'd left the Second Edition after lunch. I'd been instrumental in talking Withanee into getting something other than steel-shanked hiking boots like those that had caused so much blistering on my feet 43 years ago, and what she came up with were soft walking shoes that instead caused terrible cramping of her feet on uneven rock-packed terrain such as what they'd just crossed.

Yet another idea joined by so many discarded tactics that seemed brilliant at the time, but were peppered by unintended consequences.

After shedding their packs and catching their breath with a cold IPA Val and I offered the possibility of returning to Panamint Springs for a *real* shower and a café-type dinner, that is if they weren't too stove up. Gosh, we may as well have breathed life into a fencepost; they were on it like a rooster on a June bug. Just prior to our offer Shawn had stepped out to clear off a perimeter of rocks for a sleeping area, which he was accomplishing in a manner consistent with his day job as a Hotshot

Perhaps the Second Edition was a little more weird than the first.

wildland firefighter—that is, with enthusiasm. After the offer it was with *unbridled* enthusiasm, and before you knew it everybody was packed into the Subaru and ready to go, camping area cleared of rock and ready for their return.

Upon our arrival at Panamint Springs we parked the Subaru at our prearranged campsite while our weary hikers headed for the showers. Not too long after, the camp lighting, which had just come on, went off, followed quickly by my daughter and wife high-stepping it toward our car. They were quickly followed by Josh and Shawn who were laughing uncontrollably. It seems Withy had blown the campground circuit breaker with her high-amperage hair dryer, somehow smuggled aboard with the necessary bathing gear. We made good our getaway by driving across the highway to the restaurant area, where we hoped to regain a sense of innocence by appearing as bona fide tourists stopping in for a meal.

And why not? We were, in fact, tourists with a mission to eat off real dishes with elbow room amid frosty mugs of India Pale Ale. Except for Val who, thankfully, had never developed a taste for it but who had, like the rest of us, developed a craving for relaxation with legroom. It was a really wonderful interlude and went a long ways in lifting all of our spirits.

Arriving back at the Wildrose campsite we sat around Minnie while I read my chapter covering tomorrow's hike. I doubt we'd been more relaxed since this thing began, and for the first time I thought it might just be possible to complete the whole thing this time around also. I surely hoped so; what a downer it would be to drop out after all they'd been through.

Come to think of it, that's the exact same thought I'd had the last time I was here.

THE TRACKS OF MY TEARS

— *Withanee* —

Back at our camp spot on Wildrose, Dad read us the next day's chapter and we settled down to sleep. My dear sweet fiancé had previously scraped out a really great sleep spot for the three Sandwalkers, and as I tucked myself into my sleeping bag I took a silent inventory of my injuries. Wiggling my toes, ouch. Straightening my legs, ouch. Rolling to my side, double ouch. Breathing, ouch, *damnit*. I drifted off to a very deep sleep, at least for a couple of hours. I awoke in the pitch black to a feeling like I was suffocating. I summed it up to a bad dream about blow dryers and rolled over, mind set on going back to sleep when I felt something wet on my pillow. Not tears. Not from my hair...hmmmmm.

I wiped my face and foggily registered that something wasn't right. Was that blood???

"Oh my gosh, I'm DYING!"

Neither Shawn nor Josh stirred at my panic, so I jumped up and stumbled my way to the Minnie Winnie.

I felt so bad storming into that little motor home, rocking the boat significantly and feeling my way to the bathroom light switch while my parents were sound asleep but not for long though. I woke them up with my gasps from the bathroom. For the first time in my life, I had a bloody nose. Seems commonplace, but I really had taken some smacks to the face in all the sports I played as a kid and had never gotten one. Not knowing quite what to do, I reverted to my six-year-old self and cried out for my mommy to save me. Blood was all over everything, and I chortled and choked while she helped clean me up and sat me down on the couch. Some interesting conversation ensued while she and Dad went back and forth on the procedure for a bloody nose. Were you supposed to lean your head back? No, that can make you choke. Lean forward? To the side? Put your feet in the air and sing the National Anthem? We finally settled on me just sitting with perfect posture and waiting it out, literally holding Mango, my stuffed bear, and sniveling while they fussed around me. I am still not sure of the cause, and Mom worried that I was taking much too much Advil and made me promise not to do that anymore. I agreed, but I think we both knew I couldn't walk one mile without it, let alone the gazillion I had left. Sorry, Mom.

Finally satisfied that everything had righted itself, she tried her darndest to convince me to sleep in the Minnie Winnie for the remainder of the night so she could keep a watchful eye on me. Aren't moms great that way? I declined; I just didn't feel right sleeping warm and snuggly with my bear inside while my fellow Sandwalkers roughed it out there. I bid my parents adieu in such an elegant manner that I bet they forgot their sniveling child that had woken them up fifteen minutes prior. Trying hard not to step on Shawn's head, I made my way back into my sleeping bag. I had half a mind to wake him up so he could console me, and maybe serve him up a little scolding for not being more concerned but thought the better of it. Maybe, just maybe, I was blowing this out of proportion.

The next morning dawned unremarkably, though the canyon we slept in treated us to some purple hues that were quite lovely. I regaled Josh and Shawn with my traumatic experience the night before, and I got some sympathy to satisfy my little teddy-bear-hugging self.

We set off, heading up Wildrose Canyon, a broken-up asphalt grade that was gradual but steady. The scenery was very different from the day before, and we had a cool morning breeze that was almost pleasant. We moved along the side of the road in our little line, our cadence breaking only when we noticed two small burros across the road from us. They moved together in perfect unison; it was strange and kind of mesmerizing—I don't think I've ever seen anything like it. We stopped to watch them for a bit, reminded of Dad's story of his fellow Sandwalker, Gary Ivie. When the Original Sandwalkers encountered wild burros on their trek, Gary procured a carrot from his pack in an attempt to lure one over. When the little bugger was within arm's length, ole Gary grabbed a handful of burro mane and leapt on, before being hurled into the air and landing with a great thud and puff of dust. Once the rest of the

Follow me to Wildrose Canyon, where there is nary a rose in sight.

Sandwalkers came out of their shock, they lowered themselves to the ground next to Gary and laughed until they cried—though Gary's tears may have been for a different reason.

Dad never figured out where that carrot came from, but he did say there were a lot of jackasses there that day. Our gradual uphill turned into some steep switchbacks, that word holding a sore spot for all of us after Mt. Whitney, and the canyon turned very narrow. It got a little dicey for a couple of miles or so, and we had to tiptoe on the side of the highway that had no shoulder whatsoever. I kept praying that there wouldn't be a car coming around each blind turn that would knock us out like dominos.

We breathed a sigh of relief as we got to the top and the road widened and flattened back out. I swear, it wasn't one minute after we had reached safety that a car did, indeed, come zooming by us headed down that narrow canyon we had just stepped out of. I guess timing really is every-thing.

Soon enough our support party came scootin' on down the road behind us and pulled over to offer up some Gatorade and witty banter.

I leaned up against the Toyota and stared longingly at the back seat, taking big swigs out of my Gatorade and willing myself not to climb in and lay down. In our conversation, Mom had casually mentioned the next meal she would be serving, which also happened to be another one of my favorites: French toast. I mention this, and all of the other meals, so often in this book because food (and beer) really did become my main motivator. In order for me to continue forward, I had to take this ridiculous thing we were doing in small pieces. I couldn't handle thinking about the next day, or the finish line, or the bigger picture. All I could do was to focus on the next break, the next meal, the next beer, and get myself to that point. Once I was there, I readjusted my sights on the break after that, and so on and so forth. It may not be the most romantic way of doing things, but hey, as Popeye would say, "I am what I am and that's all that I am."

What I was, at that point in time, was hungry. Our support party tootled away, and we watched it grow smaller, wind up even more switchbacks, and roll to a dusty stop on top of a mountain overlooking the road we were trudging along. We walked a while, and I eventually broke the silence with a thought that had been taking hold of me since Mom had uttered the magic words.

"Hey guys. Can't we cut off those switchbacks and bushwhack it straight up that mountain to the motor home?"

My question was met with mostly silence and the occasional guffaw. I tried to sweeten the deal.

"Come on guys. A straight line is a shorter distance, and there is FRENCH TOAST waiting for us up there!" They laughed and kept walking, but I knew Shawn, and I also knew that I had masterfully planted a seed. Now all I needed to do was shut my mouth and wait for it to grow. Before long, he pulled out his phone and did some calculations before speaking out in agreement. Reason number 364,832,560 why I chose to spend my life with that man.

"Well. It would definitely cut off some distance, and actually, I don't think the walking would be that bad. I think we can do it."

Josh was against the idea from the onset, and I can understand why. If we stayed on the road we knew what to expect, and the uphill would be much more gradual. If we went off course and went straight up that puppy, we would have to crash our way through knee high brush and, admittedly, it did look a little steep. What he didn't factor in was French toast.

Me and the OG Sandwalker on his perch. There's never been a closer duo.

I know he thought we were crazy, but he sighed to let us know he was out-voted, and we veered off the highway and made our way up the mountain toward the motor home. Dad had himself perched on top of a large rock and had his binoculars fixed on his little protégés, who had obviously made a change in plans. When we got close enough to yell at him, I called out, "French toast!" Dad knows me so well, I could see him smile and shoot out a thumbs up, understanding full well why we strayed.

We made it to the top, and I teetered over on the rock Dad was perched on. I was pretty proud of my idea. We had cut off about a mile and a half, and even Josh admitted it was the right call. It was the first time I had really contributed to our navigation, also the last, and I almost threw my shoulder out patting myself on the back.

Maybe the saddest moment of the whole week came shortly thereafter, when Dad broke the news that there had been a change in the menu. I can't remember why, but we ended up having jambalaya for lunch instead. It was still delicious, and really, it didn't matter all that much that it wasn't my French toast. I was simply grateful that the idea got me up the hill and into a folding chair. We were nine miles into the day, and we had at least that many to go, so Shawn helped me up and we got back to it. Time was a-wastin' as they say.

Back on the road we went. There was a shoulder now, and it wasn't uphill at all. This section of the walk didn't look menacing whatsoever, but the next few hours would prove to be the most challenging for me yet, which was saying a lot. To the eyeball, everything looked flat and fairly easy in the way of walking. To the injured knee, however, there existed an inward slant to the road that required a stabilization that it no longer had. The pain was excruciating, and before I knew it, I had silent tears rolling down my cheeks. They tasted salty and full of humiliation. It was the first time I had broken down and cried in pain during The Walk, and I was ashamed of myself. Because I was bringing up the rear as usual I don't think the guys noticed, and I was really thankful for that. What a ninny.

We transitioned from Wildrose to Emigrant Pass, and finally that slant that threatened my demise slowly worked itself back upright. I was still in considerable pain, but it wasn't even in the same ballpark as it had been before. Shawn could sense something wasn't OK with me, and he draped his arm around my shoulder while hollering out to Josh, "Let's take a break! I'm tired!"

True love, I tell you.

I flopped over into the brush and hung my head in miserable shame while my cohorts tossed around encouraging words and all the positive outlooks they could come up with. We were so close, really we were, not only to the end of that day but to the end of The Walk itself. I really appreciated their positivity and tried half-heartedly to join in, but I was zapped. Shawn nudged my shoulder with his and I looked up at him. With that big ole grin I'm so darn fond of, he reached into the very depths of his pack and pulled out a Sierra Nevada Pale Ale, popped the top with the corner of his iPhone, and handed it to me. My eyes filled with tears for the second time that day, but in the most pure form of gratitude. I made a weary mental note to call to mind these moments later in life, perhaps when I want to strangle him, as I know happens in a marriage from time to time.

As we sat there, me slurping greedily on my beer, a vehicle came into view, rolled up and pulled over. It was a Bureau of Land Management, or BLM, rig. I have to admit that I felt a tidal wave of panic. I stowed my beer under my pack and shakily stood, wiping my sweaty hands on my shorts and plastering a smile on my face. Two BLM ranger-types got out of the pickup and walked our way. I guess I was nervous that (1) I had been lying on the side of the road chugging a beer and (2) I was somehow scared that we would get in some sort of trouble for being out there. You know, on "public land" that seemed to have so much red tape I wasn't 100 percent sure that it was even OK to walk across a national park. I realize this sounds harsh, and probably a little silly, especially because I worked for a federal agency and actually even worked for the BLM years ago. As much as I had hurt the last few hours though, the thought of someone shutting down this walk was much, much more painful and I couldn't bear the thought.

The ensuing conversation was so much more docile than I had envisioned, and the guys were just checking to see if we needed help and inquire as to why we were out here. I mean, were we crazy? Once we told them what we were up to and they got over the shock of such a dumb idea, they made sure we had a support party with adequate supplies (adequate, you ask? You should see our beer stock!). They were so nice that I felt bad for having jumped to conclusions so quickly. They wished us luck on our journey and took off in a cloud of dust down the highway.

That weird rush of adrenaline, probably coupled with the beer, gave me the gusto I needed to go on. I will say this, I desperately needed that encounter to remind myself just how much this whole thing meant to me. It was like the bigger picture suddenly snapped into place in my mind, and I felt the need to protect this dream with whatever I could muster up. I put away my dukes and grinned at the guys.

Walk on, Sandwalkers. Walk on.

MUST BE WILD ROSES
IN THERE SOMEWHERE

— Jim —

After we had turned in and were lost in deep sleep, I heard the motor home door open in a universe far, far away, followed by muffled feet padding past into the bathroom. It's difficult to rise to the surface like that but both Val and I did, reluctantly. Val knew it was Withanee, in the way all mothers know, and jumped out of bed. Withy came out of the bathroom holding a reddening washrag to her face while crying about a bloody nose, so Val sat her on the couch and checked her, confirming Withy's fear. I was as fully awake as I get at two o'clock in the morning so I swung my legs over the bed and, reaching deep into my old EMT training, said: "Lay down and elevate your feet, Withy."

Val, who'd taken the EMT course with me a few decades ago, shook her head: "No, that's for shock I think. If she's got a nosebleed you want to keep her head above her body."

That sounded right. Still, my advice was good for most people who'd been pounced on by sudden catastrophes, so I laid back and elevated my feet.

It helped.

Meanwhile, Val had Withanee sit up straight and tilt her head forward. She held the washrag to With's nose and gently pinched the bridge of her nose while calmly telling her she should quit taking so many Advil pain-killers for her knees, doing the stuff that mothers are so doggone good at that fathers so valiantly attempt and aren't. After 10 or 15 minutes the nosebleed stopped, and Val got Withy cleaned up and calmed down to the point where she was ready to go back to her sleeping bag. We tried to talk her into staying in Minnie for this one night, but she said no, she was determined to do this the way it was supposed to be done. There's nothing we could say except that we'd keep her in our prayers and hope for a good night's sleep from here on. However, in the back of my mind lurked the real possibility that The Walk might indeed be over, depending on how this played out. So it was hard to get back to sleep even though I was no longer in shock; that feet-elevated thing works better than you'd think.

I'd no sooner seriously closed my eyelids, it seemed, than the real alarm clock started its incessant whining and up we got again. By now we were beginning to look like a well-oiled headquarters unit; I cranked up the generator to start the morning coffeefest, Val commenced to breaking eggs in the frying pan, and our hikers began shuffling through the door as the desert sky brightened with the prospect of a brand new day. What that day would bring was entirely up to the Sandwalkers Second Edition, in large part dependent upon Withanee's condition.

She said she was fine, except for her knees and feet and such, but ready, willing, and able to trek on. And the nosebleed? She said she'd fallen right back to sleep and it never resurfaced. Apparently it came out of nowhere and returned to the same place with just that one how-do-you-do. Josh and Shawn both cast their votes in favor of carrying on and Val nodded, so it was unanimous. As they say at Cape Kennedy, "We have a go." That being said, NASA rockets will then either fire into outer space or explode in transit. If you think about it, that could fairly depict the Sandwalkers upcoming day.

And then they were off, after their customary six-finger-day photo. It didn't take much to see they really enjoyed having to hold up both hands to get the count right. I sat out in my lawn chair with my coffee again, but unlike yesterday there weren't any further insights on my part or slapstick on theirs. They just gradually went 'round the bend, so to speak, and it was a nice mundane start to the day.

Wildrose Canyon Road was a genuinely paved road in 1974, but at some point—I'm guessing after the park designation—the road was only maintained up to the nearby gate. Beyond that it had apparently been left to deteriorate, as the asphalt was broken and potholed to the point where it looked iffy for a motor home. I found that curious because there was a ranger station up in Wildrose Canyon where we OGs had stopped to check in. We'd been asked to do that so we could confirm our route into Death Valley in case they needed to come looking for us. I remember the ranger there as being a little incredulous but friendly and forthcoming with us. There was at that time—and still is—a road running down the west side of Death Valley that would have been an ideal place for our support party to meet us before we had to cross Devil's Golf Course, but it was closed to the public during the hot months. If you got in trouble out there in those days you were in real trouble, and more than a few travelers paid with their lives, just like the Valley warns with its name. The officials wouldn't make an exception even in our case, and it would nearly cost us the whole shootin' match back then.

I'd taken for granted that we could stop and chat with the ranger this time also, maybe get an update or two. It was not to be; we'd find shortly that the station had been closed down, apparently for good.

We decided to take the motor home through the canyon first. If it couldn't negotiate the road hazards we'd hopefully have enough time to turn around and loop north past Panamint Springs to take Highway 190 east and then Emigrant Canyon Road back south. We could then approach Wildrose Canyon from the opposite direction, but that would entail a 100+ mile round trip so it wasn't as if we had all day to figure this out.

Val followed in the Subaru as Winnie and I crept up the canyon, keeping the rocking motion caused by alternating potholes to a minimum. It was four winding miles to the ranger station, and the only living things we saw were our walkers, though they'd only qualify for the lower, dinged-up end of that scale. However, they seemed pretty cheerful as we passed, which was encouraging—I didn't recall seeing any of that when we walked through here—and we were able to keep on truckin', if you can call it that.

When we reached the junction of Emigrant Canyon Road I was a bit surprised; although there is now a stop sign there next to another swinging pipe gate, I'd remembered the paved road as a switchback to the left on up the canyon, but the road to the right had been unpaved for the quarter of a mile down to the ranger station and beyond. I think.

We drove down to where the ranger station used to be, and the buildings are all there as best as I remember but the rangers aren't. There aren't any signs up either, other than for a campground that I didn't remember.

Although the house and buildings are obviously kept up and probably lived in, at least intermittently, there was no information to be had around there anymore, and I didn't see anybody or any cars around.

We turned around and headed uphill to find a good spot to leave Minnie hopefully where we could get well off the highway and set up for lunch. When we passed the now-gated road, I noticed there was a stop sign bolted to the open gate, indicating the four-mile stretch of road between that gate and the one we camped near would be shut down at times. Couldn't imagine why, unless it flooded fairly often, because closing that road would add another 30 miles or so to get over the mountains from the south of Panamint Valley. We were very grateful it hadn't been closed this trip and drove on past.

The road switched back and forth for about a mile and then straightened out to a gentler uphill. This was the place where, on the original walk, we encountered a bunch or herd or flock or whatever you call a gathering of wild burros. It was memorable because Gary impulsively decided he'd try to ride one of those furry little critters. It didn't turn out well for Gary, but it still makes me smile whenever I think of it, and although I hadn't seen any burros this trip, who knows? I shuddered to think my daughter might try to replicate that part of our trip.

We set up on the top of a hill about 5 miles from there, above a second set of switchbacks that I was sure our walkers would enjoy, and rode the Subaru back to get Yoda. On our return we stopped and took a break with our hikers, and far in the distance you could see the motor home on top of that hill. I wasn't sure if that white speck up there cheered or depressed them, or me for that matter. They all hurt to varying degrees with my daughter being the clear frontrunner, and although even her smile hurt she gave me a big one, and began hobbling off toward that little white speck. It was getting really, really difficult to drive away and leave her like that.

We'd leveled our lunch wagon in a nice wide clearing, and because the breeze was calm we were able to unfurl the attached awning for shade. That done I found a nice rock outcropping over near the edge to use for a perch where I could cheer on the Sandwalkers, when they got within cheering range. That might take awhile I thought as I watched the tiny figures through binoculars. They'd stop every now and then, huddle and point at our hill, and continue along the road until they suddenly swerved off the highway and started directly toward us. They were obviously going to cut out the upcoming switchbacks and climb straight up the hill. They'd learned the same lesson we had when it came to highway switchbacks; because the inward part of the curves are slanted it's horrible on the ankles and knees. Good for them for bypassing that misery, and they'd whittle off some mileage to boot. The drawback, of course, was the steepness you encounter by doing that, but it's a good trade. Usually. All mountains get steeper toward the top until you reach the tipping point where it starts leveling out near the summit, which is where I was perched. Switchbacks, when you're walking, are just naturally employed 'cause your ankle joints don't hinge far enough to keep you going upright straight-line, but self-made switchbacks are a lot less stressful than those engineered for highways.

As they closed Withanee switched on back right over to me and gave me the best hug I've ever had, returned in kind. Josh and Shawn were right behind her, with high-fives and tricky fist-bumps, and we retired to the motor home for another great lunch whipped up by Val in my absence, somehow. Afterward we enjoyed slices of cold watermelon beneath the awning, with high hopes of a strong finish for the day, or at least a survivable finish. However, when they started walking again, well, even the latter began to appear optimistic.

And if that wasn't enough there was a major change in the works for tonight: we wouldn't be retracing the original Sandwalkers route. Ever since we left the gated rose-less Wildrose Canyon we'd officially been on Emigrant Canyon Road, with Emigrant Pass topping out a little over 2 miles north of our hilltop lunch area. Just beyond that, perhaps half a mile, we OGs had hiked east up Wood Canyon Road to the top of the Panamint Mountains where we'd made our last camp before descending into Death Valley. Val and I had scouted the route in the 4Runner a few weeks ago and found the Wood Canyon Road, which starts out just dandy, turns into another "day use only" area and slowly deteriorates into no road at all a mile short of the saddle where we'd camped in '74. That mile is impassable without four-wheel drive, and we barely clawed our way up there even with four-wheel drive. In order for us to take this route we'd have to camp a good two and a half miles below the saddle, which the Second Edition would then have to hike before beginning a very steep, rocky, dangerous descent into Trail Canyon below. We'd barely made it back then, leaving from the camp at the top. Today? Very, very doubtful you could safely climb down our old route after fighting your way up the steep and rocky incline to the top.

When Val and I originally saw this, I thought that was the end of Withanee's dream of making this journey, but we looked at the map and saw another possible route about a mile farther up Emigrant Canyon Road. It was Aguereberry Point Road, and it was also a "day use only" road, but the road east was maintained all the way past several canyon heads that dropped into Trail Canyon, the only passable route into Death Valley from this area. If the Second Edition could take one of these, they would rejoin the OG route when they spilled into Trail Canyon. We found what appeared to be a good route down into Trail Canyon in a tributary canyon about 5 miles east of the paved Emigrant Canyon Road. It wouldn't be an easy walk—surprise, surprise, huh?—because the maintained part of the dirt road coming up through the canyon was in places pretty darn miserable, but it was passable in a carefully driven car so it was better than anyplace else we'd seen. And the drop into Trail Canyon was certainly much better than the one from Woods Canyon, so. . . .

All of this was of course backstory to the Second Edition because we'd gone over this a number of times, but like all the rest of The Walk they'd never seen any of it before, and reality always differs intensely from what you imagine.

But for today the "Day Use Only" sign on Aguereberry Point Road would be our campsite one last time, and Val and I busied ourselves getting the motor home in shape for our charges when they arrived.

This was about the time, they told me later, they'd encountered BLM rangers. I don't think it's a stretch to relate their meeting with uniformed park officials in Death Valley to our meeting with a uniformed park official on Mt. Whitney. You can't deny there's some kind of an equation with this back and forth stuff so closely aligned between this trip and the original trip. It was getting a little creepy, especially to a father who, because of OG Gary, was trying to suppress the prospect of his exhausted daughter hopping onto the back of a wild burro.

AND SARSAPARILLA
TAKES THE LEAD

— *Withanee* —

We met up with our support partiers after turning right onto Aguereberry Road. We recounted them with the last few hours of stories, had a snack (well, I did. It was a slice of lemon cake and it was delectable), and took off. We meandered through the desert and the ghost town of Harrisburg, which was pretty neat. Named after Shorty Harris, who had staked a gold claim there with his friend Pete Aguereberry in 1906, Harrisburg became home to several hundred miners for a brief time while they all worked to strike it rich. We walked past an old mill called "Cashiers Mill" and a couple of rock walls as well as obvious outlines of miner dwellings. I love ghost towns because they feel ever-so-mysterious, and I entertained myself by creating backstories for the miners that soap opera networks would be proud of.

Keeping my mind busy was a challenge, but if I didn't focus on something other than the pain, it threatened to swallow me whole. I found myself quietly staring at my aching feet shuffling below me as I fell farther and farther behind my fellow Sandwalkers, searching my brain for a new life preserver to grab hold of.

I started thinking about my dear ol' dad, who was waiting for me somewhere in the distance, and his journey in 1974. Somehow that thought funneled into a memory of a weird phenomenon he experienced once, during which he focused all his energy into throwing one leg out in front of the other.

"Well, Dad," I had said when he regaled me with his tale, "that really just sounds like...normal walking."

"No, no no no no."

He claimed that throwing everything he had into that one swing of his leg, and then doing it again and again, propelled him forward at warp speed. Not only that, but it took a slight edge off the pain because, again, all of his attention and energy went into the high kick.

Well, that seemed simple enough.

Since I had nothing else to do, I figured I would give her a go.

Cowabunga! I swung my right leg out as hard as I could, as fast as I could. Then with the left. Wasn't so bad, so I did it again. Before I could really understand what was happening, I almost caught up with Josh and Shawn. I squeezed between them, zoned in on each kick-step, and flew on by. I had to bend over a little at the waist to see my new rocket feet perform, so I imagine I looked, well, a little nuts. The guys hadn't heard me coming up behind them, and I think they both jumped a little as I passed 'em up like a dirty shirt.

I opened my mouth to take another measured breath when a weird horse race caller voice came booming out of me, yelling, "And Sarsaparilla takes the lead!"

I hardly registered their shock, but I did feel them pick up speed though to no avail. They couldn't catch me, *nosiree,* and this would be the first and only time they would ever eat my dust. It was downright invigorating, and I was able to hold this pace for quite a while, only breaking concentration to ask Shawn how many miles we had left to our support party. Initially, he had called out from the dust cloud behind me, "Two! Two more miles!" I could tell he was breathing hard, and I gave myself a mental high five. Two more miles, no problem. Kick-step, kick-step, kick-step. Breathe. Kick-step, kick-step, kick-step. The sound of Sarsaparilla's gait sure was hypnotizing. I guess the best way to describe this moment is what people call a "runner's high." Though I run often now, 500 miles total last calendar year, I've never experienced a feeling even close to the one I got that day. It was amazing, and if I could bottle it up and sell it, I would be richer than Scrooge McDuck.

I heard a noise and soon realized that a car was coming down the road behind us. I scooted over to let it pass, but I didn't slow my new-found pace. As it bumped along the road past me, I saw what it was. A silver convertible.

A silver convertible.

A silver convertible, with the top down.

It was shocking to see *any* vehicle out here, but this one took the cake. I side-eyed them as they drove by, scared to lose concentration on my turbo legs, but saw enough that the memory will last me for years to come. They were definite city-folk, a man driving and a young blond sitting next to him with her mouth pursed, presumably to avoid sucking in dust. She didn't look the least bit amused, and I couldn't blame her. The road was not good—washed out and rocky—and I had heard it would get much worse ahead. The sight was too much for me. I was somewhat maniacal at that point, and laughing wildly at myself. I hollered back at Josh and Shawn, "This is no place for a convertible!"

That line may have been lost on these guys, but man, my dad would have *howled*. Since I was old enough to remember, there was one movie that he played over and over and over, to the point where we could quote most of it pretty darn well before I graduated high school. Mom got so disgusted with him that she would always seem to hear the phone ringing, or the dryer stop, or something else that needed her urgent attention every time he put it on.

What movie, you may ask? Why, none other than that 1963 comedy with an all-star cast, *It's a Mad, Mad, Mad, Mad World,* in which Phil Silvers attempts to drive his Ford Coupe convertible through ridiculous terrain to try to get to a buried load of cash before anyone else. As he crosses a river and starts to sink, he yells out to a kid standing on the bank in a very New England–type accent, "This is no place for a convoitable!"

Cut to Sasparilla.

Josh and Shawn thought I had totally cracked by this point, but I didn't care. I was soaring up that road, which narrowed a little and wound its way up another, you guessed it, canyon. The footing was getting increasingly worse, and the serrated edges of pain were starting to creep back in. I hollered back at Shawn, thinking this *had* to be near the two-mile mark, but I couldn't see the red Toyota, and I was getting suspicious.

I could hear the remorse in Shawn's voice when he said back, "Um, I think I might have miscalculated the mileage before. . . ."

WHAT!?

This pin deflated my balloon and fast. It's still up for debate here how many miles he had been short, but it was *most certainly* more than 2 miles.

As much as I love that man, I felt betrayed.

I tried to will my kick-steps to continue, and they did, for a little while. But after Shawn's confession, I started to weaken, and I felt the moleskin/band-aid sock on the inside of my foot slip ever so slightly. I told myself to ignore it, focus on the high kick, but a few more steps and that sucker was off completely. Whahhhhhhh.

I came to a screeching halt, with every piece of my body on fire and ice-cold, simultaneously. I leaned backward and fell right on over onto my pack, like a turtle onto its shell.

That, right there, is something I never remember my dad telling me. The benefits of his technique were undeniable, but it comes at a price. And it's a steep one.

The guys caught up to me as I was yanking off my pink shoes and dirt-lined socks. My blister was angry, and so was I. I read my future husband the riot act, right there on the side of Aguereberry Road. I know he didn't tell me the wrong distance on purpose. This man, along with my brother, basically carried me 131 miles in the most miserable condition of my life. But in that moment, I coulda' strangled him. I thought back to what he said on Mt. Whitney. Lows are low, indeed.

Every square inch of my body hurt. I felt muscles seizing that I never even knew existed. It was time to pay the piper for my moment of greatness, with interest.

My guys helped me figure out my moleskin sock and finally pulled me upright. I limped behind them in pouty silence for another mile or so when we finally closed in on the hill where Dad's little red Toyota was sitting. Sarsaparilla had been put out to pasture as abruptly as she had come out the gate, and the flies were a swarmin', by golly.

We got to our support party, and I heaved a sigh of relief as I ripped off my shoes and reached out my grubby little hand for a beer before uttering a word. We had conquered a little more than 17 painful miles, effectively completing day number 6. Praise be to God.

We had to drive back down to our night's campsite as we weren't allowed to camp atop of Aguereberry Point, per the BLM's regulations for the national park. We did spend a little time up there though—the guys relaxing, and me whining—and all having ourselves a little sudsy medicine. It was so surreal to think that in 24 hours or less, we would have completed The Walk. Tears filled my eyes for the third time that day. Wow, what a feeling. What. A. Feeling.

A BETTER ROUTE, THEORETICALLY

—*Jim*—

We parked Minnie Winnie as close as possible to the "Day Use Only beyond This Point" sign on the Aguereberry Point Road turnout and got everything in some semblance of order before our walkers arrived. Afterward I climbed up on the roof where I perched with my binoculars and was finally rewarded with our little stick figures turning from the highway about a half-mile south, and then heading off into the desert parallel to our road. They were obviously trying to whittle off some more mileage by cutting off the road's loop around a low hill lying some distance off to our southeast. There's no denying the wisdom in that, and while I applauded the idea, I, for some perfectly sound reason I'm sure, called them on the radio and asked that they come by the motor home in lieu of their shortcut.

So they did.

I wish I could remember why it was I asked, but I can't.

And what's worse, *they* can't.

While writing this two years after The Walk, I called my daughter at her home in Carson City and asked why in the world I would have called them over that miserably hot, dusty memorable-only-because-of-the-Walk day and she said, "What? I thought we came over because I was hungry. I do remember the wonderful lemon bars, but. . .nope, got nothing for you on that."

She then checked with her husband Shawn, who was her fiancé during The Walk, and he didn't recall anything either other than the misery part of it. Withy then called her Sandwalker brother Josh, who now lives in Texas, and he didn't have any recollection of that shortcut being short-circuited either.

They did, however, have their route traced and stored on their phone thingies, and they all found it curious that their route—displayed as a red line—made a distinct and unexplained detour to the left a few hundred yards after leaving the highway. It went over to where we'd set up the motor home and then *looped back* to their original route to the south of the hill where, incidentally, the ghost town of Harrisburg was located. It clearly showed a detour from the planned route, which probably added at least a half mile to their walk that day, but none of us can remember or explain why.

Curious, because you do not, ever, add even one extra step to a hike of that magnitude without a clear and present reason that could pass muster with a master tactician, let alone an OG who'd been out in the sun all day.

Well. Since there can now be no resolution, I suppose we'll have to call it one of those decisions so grand and obvious that nobody involved has the slightest idea what it might have been. That's got to be the best kind, no doubt about it, so I thank me with all my heart and hereby graciously accept all the adulation due myself. With an aside to Val, of course, for the lemon bars that everyone does seem to remember.

After they stepped back off into their interrupted shortcut Val and I locked up Minnie and headed out in Yoda, stocked with plenty of ice, drinks, and maps. The dirt road was fairly straight for a couple of miles and then joined the convoluted twisting terrain so common in these parts. From that point it was another 3 miles up to where we'd turn from Aguereberry Road for perhaps another hundred yards up to the saddle marking the head of the canyon we'd scouted and decreed was passable. More on that shortly, but for now the plan was to meet the walkers there and pick them up, since overnight camping wasn't allowed up there. We'd then drive them back to our motor home campsite and bring them back up at first light tomorrow, when they'd start the last day of their trek down into Death Valley.

It seemed like a good plan, and that was starting to worry me, so perhaps I was getting the hang of this stuff after all; good plans between Mt. Whitney and Death Valley had a proven tendency to take unforeseen severe and lasting lumps.

At top of the saddle the road was blocked by another gate, as the old road itself had at one time gone on down the western wall of the canyon. That was before a section of it had slid off the mountainside and rendered it impassable about a quarter of a mile beyond. They certainly didn't need a gate to keep me from driving on down, but I suppose there are Evel Knievel types who might give it a go. Not to mention wayward and foolish hikers on foot, which of course we wouldn't mention if our lives depended on it.

The walkers took longer than I expected and when they finally turned onto the approach road below they looked rather ragged. Withanee in particular looked like she ought to be in a wheelchair, leaning heavily and using her legs like they were anchors rather than propellers, which they had obviously become.

She barely made it to Yoda before her anchors plumb gave out, and it took me and Shawn and Josh and Val to lift her onto the tailgate gently enough to keep her from hollering. This is tough stuff for parents and brothers and fiancés, but altogether now. . . .

The Second Edition of the Sandwalkers were fading, but they were also smiling, every one of them. I, more than any, should know why. But it is hard to watch your loved ones going through such a difficult, miserable, debilitating time and know that you, personally, are the one responsible for it. In my defense, I had no idea my spectacular lack of sense all those many years ago would trickle down for a generation, or perhaps even longer. It was like lighting a long, long fuse. Lordy, dynamiters have to know where, exactly, a fuse is going when they light it. That should be a firm requirement for those who might in their future become fathers; veins of gold-bearing quartz have little value when compared to children.

On the flip side of that, when your own people honor you with something like what the Second Edition was doing in my name, it is no doubt the highest honor that can be given. That sort of honor isn't bestowed easily or without a whole lot of pain. It is the sharpest example of a two-edged sword I've ever encountered.

From where we sat on the saddle above Death Valley, we didn't have a great view of the valley itself, although we could make out the white salt flats far to the south through a small V on the left. However, the slope descending toward Trail Canyon was much more gradual than anything we'd seen to this point, which was a very good thing indeed.

We loaded up Yoda and headed back to the motor home, and while negotiating back through the narrow, rocky canyon, Josh and Shawn told us of Withanee's rocketing pace for close to 3 miles in which she severely road-runnered her two coyote tag-alongs.

What? The daughter we had to lift onto the tailgate? That one? Yes, they said.

"She *galloped* past us, hollering 'and Sarsparilla takes the lead!' We had an awful time trying to catch up—never did actually, until she gave out, thank God."

I looked back at my daughter, and she gave me a sheepish grin that I'd come to know as, "Yes, I did. Sorry." Come to find out she recalled a reading from my book a couple nights ago where I recounted Glenn's running into "the wall," a physical/mental barrier encountered by endurance runners. Glenn had broken through it by throwing his legs out beyond the pain, which is much easier said than done, and when he recounted it I gave it a try, and by George it worked. It's like buying stamina on credit though, and when you finally give out, well, you quickly become bankrupt and your muscles freeze up like rusty bolts, loosening an avalanche of pain that is dang near unbearable as Withy could now attest, chip off the old block that she is.

She also told me of the convertible that passed them and how she used one of our favorite lines from my favorite movie, *It's a Mad, Mad, Mad, Mad World,* which caused me to laugh so hard my eyes teared up, and I came near to running us off the road. Laughter like that is contagious, you know, and although our other three passengers were woefully ignorant of the humor's origin, they, too, got caught up in our narrative: "This is no place for a convoitable!" (howl howl) "This is *way* no place for a convoitable!"

Side-splitting stuff, let me tell you, which Withy probably didn't need at that particular moment. Her hilarity was very often punctuated with "ouch."

When we came chuckling back to Minnie Winnie, there was barely enough daylight left for Shawn to carve out a sleeping area behind the motor home. After everybody was cleaned up, and Val had served another great meal, we sat around while I read the chapter concerning our final day of The Walk 43 years ago.

It was finally sinking in that tomorrow would be the grand finale. Tomorrow we would either cross the finish line or come up short. But The Walk would be over. Tomorrow.

Wow.

INTO THE VALLEY OF DEATH

— *Withanee* —

Spirits were high, probably because of the high amount of spirits. I had all but forgotten the misery I had endured that day, and as we bumped and dipped back down the very rugged Aguereberry Road, we all roared with laughter as the story of Sarsaparilla was recounted. We ended the night with foot baths, dinner in the form of what my mom fondly calls "beanie weenies," and went off to bed, dreaming of that finish line the next day. Lying in my sleeping bag, I promised myself that I'd either do it or die trying. And I meant it.

Day 7 didn't dawn as jovially as I would have hoped. I was stressed, limping around, and getting my pack lined out as my dad worked to cut out my moleskin and gather the other assorted medical supplies it took just to get me upright anymore. Every morning, Dad and Shawn would go to work bandaging up my owwies, because (1) they are incredible fellas and (2) I always seemed to mess it up if I tried it myself. Meanwhile, Joshy would work on all of his various blisters, some of the biggest I have ever seen in my life. I somehow managed to be ready to leave, but as I crawled my way into the 4Runner, I realized my foot bandages—an intricate pattern of moleskin, band-aids, and duct tape—wasn't sitting right on my foot. We had a thirty-minute drive up to Aguereberry Point to start our morning, and we were trying to leave in time to get to walking while it was still dark and relatively cool. I knew it would be an unwise choice to try to tackle that day without giving my feet some kind of fighting chance, but I still mentally argued back and forth. I mentioned to my dad that something was going awry inside my shoe, and he insisted we go back to the motor home, prop my foot up and redo it. All this foolery took us an extra 20 to 30 minutes to fix, putting us late, late for this very important date.

I felt guilty as we rattled up the road, but my foot sure didn't. Thankfully, it ended up not being an error in bandage adhesive that had us running so late, but rather, a very special gift from The Big Guy. As we unloaded our gear for the day, the sun began to rise and we were treated to the most spectacular sunrise I have ever, and probably will ever, see. The mountains surrounding us were washed in oranges and pinks, and wayyyyyyyyyyyyy down below all that, we could darn near see our end point. The thought of that had us, in a word, giddy.

The giddiness wasn't confined to the walkers though. Mom and Dad were in the middle of it all, hyped to the gills. The energy on top of that mountain that morning was somethin' else, I tell you, and the combination of the view, cool temperature, and unbelievable fact that we were so *darned close* we could all taste it made us drunk with excitement. I venture to say that even the crisp, new shirts we were wearing played an important role in the group's mood that morning.

I had the shirts made earlier that month and presented each Sandwalker with one at the start of the trip. The three walkers' read, "Sandwalkers, Second Edition. Mt. Whitney to Death Valley, 2017." Mom and Dad's said, "Sandwalkers, Mt. Whitney to Death Valley, 2017" and then on the back, "We put the party in Support Party!" I also went a little extra and made Dad a second shirt with "OG Sandwalkers, 1974" listing the names of all four of the Originals. I had beer koozies made with the same logos, and those things came in handy throughout that week. I guess I've never been accused of *under*doing things.

Anyway, I had decided I wanted to make shirts months before but had gotten really busy with the 2017 fire season. Before I could create my design, I left for a work assignment to a fire near Brookings, Oregon, for fourteen days. All of a sudden, the window in which everything seemed totally doable—design shirts, get shirts ordered, shirts get created and then sent out to me—was getting smaller and smaller. I remember being so busy on that fire that I sketched out the design on a napkin, took a blurry picture of it with my cell phone, and emailed it to a company called Big Frog in Reno. They executed it perfectly, and Josh was able to swing by and pick them up on the night before we left for Mt. Whitney. Whew.

The shirts were made of some cotton-poly blend that allowed moisture to wick off them, and I had been ready to wear mine all week in that darn

Last morning giddiness.

The best parents a girl could ask for.

heat, but Josh and Shawn had another idea. They wanted to wait until the last day—having actually *earned* them. And man, were we about to.

We snapped some photos in our new digs with the world's most beautiful backdrop and started off one last time, just a-grinnin'.

As we started down the mountain, 17 miles from our final destination, Mom and Dad began serenading their Sandwalkers one last time with the infamous Roy Rogers song "Happy Trails."

And just like that, I was crying. *Again.*

Due to our support party's diligent scouting months prior, we took a different canyon down to the alluvial fans than the Original Sandwalkers had, one that ran parallel to where their footprints are embedded forever.

The OGs were probably the first and only fools to walk there, too. They took Emigrant Pass to the head of Trail Canyon, which by name is deceiving. The only trail they were lucky enough to slide down was one the burros had worn, kinda. As we wound our way down our path, we kept stealing glances across where they had come down and I have to say, it made the Canyon of Horrors look somewhat mild. All we could really see were sheer rock cliffs and what looked to be totally unmanageable terrain. True OGs, those guys. We all marveled at their toughness and fortitude for the umpteenth time that week.

Eventually we came to the jeep trail that I supposed Trail Canyon was named for. It was only mid-morning, and it was already hot. The footing was rocky, and each step was a millimeter more painful than the step before, yet a millimeter closer to the end—if you are a glass half full type. I never loved that saying. I guess it's because the only thing I care about is what's in the glass. Is it Budweiser, 'cause if so, count me *out*. In all fairness, I had been warned about the heat, so I brought with me an extra gallon of a water/Gatorade mix. Exactly as my dad had before me, unfortunately, I drank every drop before we even made it to the salt flats. Josh and Shawn were so great though; their excitement was contagious, even when the going was tough. They even shared some of their water with me.

The guys had been talking about how Shawn's favorite team, the Buffalo Bills, were playing that morning and he was dying to know the score. Too bad for him though that we hadn't had cell phone service since somewhere around Lone Pine, five days prior. I have been to Death Valley many a time, I'll tell you, and there has never been an ounce of a signal out there. Josh, being almost as good of a friend as he is a brother, tried anyway, I guess for the sake of saying he did. I'll be darned, too, if he wasn't able to magically pick up the very final minutes of the Bills game. Seeing this as a golden opportunity, I asked to stop so, *ahem*, Shawn could give the game his full attention. In all reality, I couldn't go another step because my band-aid was sliding off again. I redid my feet while Shawn and Josh hung on every word of the game. Something big happened, there was yelling, and next thing I knew there was some serious dance moves happening around me. I was lucky enough to catch the latter on video, and it's one of my most treasured captures of The Walk.

Not too shortly thereafter, I heard a crackle on my radio for another delightful treat. Our support party was now able to talk to us by direct line of sight radio, and they had oodles of good news to share. The first of which was that my aunt and family had driven down from Austin to be there waiting for us at the end. I still can't believe they did that; it meant so much to me, and I was a little bit in disbelief until she and my uncle Roger came across the radio.

"Hey there girl. Are ya doin' OK up thar?"

My uncle has a voice that sounds exactly like Boomhauer from *King of the Hill* and I absolutely love it. My aunt Shell, Uncle Roger, and cousin Gunner were all there, having joined up with my parents, and they were all waiting eagerly for us to cross the proverbial finish line of the lowest point in the continental US. I couldn't wait to see them.

After some witty banter and an appropriate dosage of heckling, my mom took the radio back over with some more good news. As a surprise, they had gotten us a hotel room that night in Death Valley. An unnecessary expense, as they had not only rented a motor home, purchased all of the food and supplies, and bought all of the *beer* for the week—and I know that wasn't cheap. What a treat! Heck with Shell and family, I couldn't wait to see that room!

That pick-me-up propelled me forward for another couple of miles, and sooner or later we wandered out to the Westside Road. This road had been closed when my dad had done The Walk, and even though he all but begged the BLM, they wouldn't consider opening it for their support party. Boy, did I get lucky. As I'm told, Uncle Roger and Dad were out doing something or other, and Roger just happened to look over and exclaim to my dad that the road he had said numerous times was closed was in fact *not*. This allowed our support party to bring over some food, precious water that I for one desperately needed, and the most ice-cold and delicious watermelon ever known to Sandwalkers.

Coming into Westside Rd, the guys looking great, and then, there's me.

As we sat and enjoyed our spoils, my navigators did some mapping on Shawn's phone to try to find that elusive "lowest spot" we needed to be sure to walk to. All that seemed to be left in this miserable, painful, totally insane journey was 3 miles. *Three.* I couldn't grasp that concept of finality. One hundred and twenty some odd miles behind us, and only three to go. A breath in the wind. Shoot, anyone could walk 3 miles if they absolutely had to! Yeah!

The thing of it is . . . and there always is a thing, isn't there? The thing of it is, the last few miles of our journey were the absolute toughest terrain of all. Tougher than the slanted highways. Tougher than that Godforsaken nightmare of a canyon. Tougher than the 22 miles up and back down Mt. Whitney. Somewhere deep in my mind I knew that fact, but I wouldn't let it creep to the front. I couldn't. I just munched on my watermelon and stared as it dribbled down my shin and into my sock.

D-DAY

—Jim—

Done-Day dawned before dawn even thought about it, the darkness outside still getting darker, as in "'tis always darkest before the dawn." It was the earliest we'd gotten up since Mt. Whitney, not because we'd become so keen on early rising but because it would take an extra 20 minutes or so to transport our charges up to their starting point. We thought this an excellent way to outsmart this built-in delay, apparently having learned nothing at all over the past week.

At first it worked to perfection, enjoying breakfast as we prepared the walkers for one more really, really horrible day. We worked especially hard on Josh's knee and Withanee's feet and knees and were actually a little ahead of the clock when we climbed into Yoda in the still morning air, ready to go.

For a moment.

Then Withanee said the repairs to her feet had inexplicably come loose, that she wouldn't be able to go on like that. So back in the Minnie Winnie we went and started all over again, which, of course, took a little more than the 20 minutes we had so cleverly saved.

Therefore dawn, unwilling to wait for us, was indeed dawning as we started driving up Aguereberry Point Road. By the time we backed into our egress point on the ridge above Trail Canyon, the east-facing flanks of the Panamint Range were catching the first golden rays of the sun. A more breathtaking morning may have been seen somewhere on Earth over the course of history, but certainly not by any of us. We took several pictures, but they never truly depicted God's handiwork we saw on the mountain that morning.

The Sandwalkers Second Edition lined up for a final seven-day finger pose, outfitted in their Sandwalker shirts, before starting down the last long leg into Death Valley proper, then turned and hiked into the painting that has since embedded itself in my mind. While they were still in earshot Val and I belted out a loud and ragged version of "Happy Trails to You," sending them off with the same tune that'd echoed into Death Valley forty-three years ago. We watched and occasionally waved back until they disappeared. By then the sunrise was complete, nearly, so we drove back to pack up our motor home for the last "official" time. The Walk was, one way or another, nearing its climax, and for Val and me, so was The Ride, thank goodness.

I drove Minnie down the winding Emigrant Canyon Road, followed closely by Val in the Subaru, until we rejoined Highway 190 near the head of an alluvial fan that spills out into Death Valley and, not coincidentally, into the small oasis of Stovepipe Wells. We left Minnie in the store parking lot all by herself while Val drove me back to get Yoda. By then it was starting to get hot, which I duly noted by rolling the rear window down, which was Yoda's only air-conditioning system. However, this was October 1, so it wasn't near as hot as it could have been, small comfort as that is, when your shirt is sticking to your back. Could have been worse, I thought; I could have been walking (hang in there, Second Edition).

From Stovepipe Wells we leapfrogged Minnie down to our last campsite at Furnace Creek Campgrounds on the other side of the valley about 26 miles southeast. Furnace Creek Ranch and Inn was undergoing a complete renovation and was pretty much shut down for the time being. The campground was still open, along with the gas station and room rentals, but everything else, other than a temporary restaurant, was fenced off. Having no store to speak of we stocked up at Stovepipe Wells before bringing Yoda down and rented a full hookup for Minnie at the campground. We were just finishing up when Val's sister Michelle and her husband Roger and son Gunner joined us. They'd driven over from their home in Austin, Nevada, to be there at the finish of The Walk, so we decided to head on down to Devil's Golf Course to await the grand finale.

We all piled into Minnie with me driving and Roger on the front passenger seat, which would turn out to be significant very shortly. About 15 minutes later, actually, as we were tooling south on Badwater Road, Roger asked me what that road was we just passed on his side. Knowing the area well I was able to reply without looking, "That's Westside Road. It crosses the valley and loops way south before crossing back over. I've never been on it because it's always locked."

"Well, it isn't locked now," Roger said, "the gate's wide open."

What? Couldn't be. I'd been through here maybe three dozen times, the latest just a couple weeks ago, and that road was *never* open. Even when we begged them to let our support party meet us at the junction of Westside Road and Trail Canyon Road back in 1974, so our support party could bring us water, they wouldn't budge. Too many people had perished over there after breaking down or getting stuck, and it'd been off limits forever, basically. I explained all that to poor old Roger and all he said was, "Well, it's open now."

I looked at him.

Badwater Road is a narrow, paved, two-lane highway with very small shoulders, not someplace you'd want to turn a motor home around on. However, on the very slim chance that Roger wasn't delusional, I managed, with a lot of short spurts of forward, reverse, forward, reverse, forward, reverse ad nauseam to get Minnie headed north again. And there, for Pete's sake, was Westside Road with the great hinged pipe-gate locked in the wide open position. No "Road Closed" signs, no nail strips thrown across the roadway, nothing to indicate you couldn't just drive on out there.

Well.

Well, well.

Withy answered on the first try with the walkie-talkie, and she said they were probably an hour or two above Westside Road and "yes-we'd-love-to-meet-you-if-that's possible-'cause-we're-running-low-on-water-and-my-feet-are-pert'near-to-fall-off, and . . .' she just kept going seemingly without taking a breath, but the point had been made: We needed to get out there and do our support party thing, but the motor home was not equipped to take some sketchy road across a place labeled "Devil's Golf Course," so we'd have to go get Yoda. Again.

We went back to the campground, loaded up Yoda with everything within reach, and Val and I headed for Westside Road. Roger, Shell, and Gunner followed in Minnie and went sailing on past when we turned off on Westside Road. They were to meet us at the Devil's Golf Course viewing area some 5 miles farther on, after our rendezvous with the walkers.

The Westside Road was in pretty good shape in some places but made up for it in others, apparently spurred to harshness whenever the salt crystals demanded, which was more often than Val and I would have liked. Even with wheels on a graded roadway the place was unfriendly, and why that should surprise me after having stumbled across it on foot is in itself surprising. Happily though, Trail Canyon was only about 5 miles down the road.

Our timing couldn't have been better; the walkers were perhaps a quarter mile away when we parked at Trail Canyon, giving us just enough time to put out some chairs and cut slices of ice-cold watermelon.

Josh and Shawn kept somewhat upright as they approached, but my daughter looked very much like she was just dragging herself along on sheer will power.

Until she saw the watermelon. All of a sudden she was just there, taking a large bite while dropping into a chair. Shawn and Josh were a nano-second behind her, all three drifting for the moment into bliss as the melon quickly disappeared. You could feel the sighs of contentment more than hear them, and we just sat around for a bit while they relaxed, as much as they could.

It dawned on me, as I sat alongside and gazed across the valley, that I'd never before been here in the daylight. The one and only time I came through here was just at dusk when we original Sandwalkers spilled out of Trail Canyon all those many years ago. In our minds we had worked out the perfect manner to cross the infamous Death Valley, which, as any fool knows, should not be attempted in the heat of a summer day. To that end we'd timed our last hike from Emigrant Gap to the valley's edge so we'd get here exactly when we actually did, with just enough daylight left to set up a dry camp. The bright idea was to sleep here until dawn when we'd saddle up and head across at first light, in the relative coolness of the morning. Is that not genius? Oh, there were a few drawbacks—one was that we'd have to carry our sleeping bags in addition to a lot of extra water, and another was that we had no way to scout a decent campsite, so our choice would be limited to whatever might do before darkness fell. But to make a long story short, which I hardly ever do, as it turned out we drank most of our water long before we reached Westside Road, and there wasn't going to be enough to stay there until morning, so after some arguing and whatnot we started into Devil's Golf Course about the same time as the night dropped a heavy curtain of black velvet around us. Without our little disposable flashlights we would have been totally blind as well as incredibly dumb, but that's another story altogether (the title of that book is *Sometimes a Great Notion . . . isn't, so much,* which was certainly appropriate).

But getting back to this trip; we did a little first aid tweaking, which probably wasn't going to help very much at this point, and our walkers started out resolutely again, angling a little to the south of a far distant dot that I was pretty sure was Minnie, parked at the viewing area while doubling as the Nineteenth Hole at this particular golf course. You couldn't see the salt pinnacles from our Trail Canyon vantage point, but they were out there just waiting to sink their little coral-like teeth into anybody foolish enough to venture into their midst.

"You guys be careful out there!" I hollered one more time. Some pearls of deep wisdom bear repeating, you know?

The line they were taking looked too far to the right to me, but Shawn's electronic gadget showed the lowest point out beyond the direction they were headed, so I assumed they were probably being guided better than we'd been—all we'd had were USGS topographical maps that showed not only the marked –282' point at Badwater Basin but two other "lowest" sites farther north and west of there. When we originally walked to the lowest point, we were plotting from the map that showed one of those sites about half a mile southeast of the Devil's Golf Course parking area situated right out in the salt pinnacles. So if Shawn had something that purported to show exactly where one of the lowest points was, he would at least have a more precise bearing than we'd had. And that's important if you're going to spend a week walking from the highest point in the 48 states to the lowest point in the Western Hemisphere, you want to end up at the honest-to-goodness lowest point and not something that's "close." Otherwise the entire thing becomes a sham, a joke, and all those blisters and hurts and aches are for nothing at all. There's not many people I know of who would settle for that.

Val and I watched until our hikers merged into the distorting heat waves, and then we retraced Westside Road back to the Badwater highway. From there it was only 5 miles (I can say "only" 5 miles because I was in a car) to Devil's Golf Course Road, which protruded a mile out into the valley and terminated at a well-maintained parking lot, its surface packed solid with salt and dirt.

Roger had Minnie Winnie parked at the far end of the lot, and they hadn't yet seen any hint of anybody anywhere, let alone walking out there in the pinnacles. We joined them, and to get a better perspective I climbed up on the roof with my binoculars, certain I could locate them because I knew their general direction from Trail Canyon. I found the Trail Canyon Road all right, and from there panned slowly left for a mile or two beyond where they had any chance of being, and darned if Roger wasn't right again: no sign of anybody, anywhere. Back and forth and near and far I scanned, but the entire valley seemed disturbingly vacant.

Well there'd been nothing easy about this trip, and apparently nothing was going to be made easy just for us today either, so we sat down to wait it out. A half hour of that was all it took for sweat to begin running down into my eyeballs, which merged the willowy heat waves into the Jabberwocky poem from Lewis Carroll's *Through the Looking-Glass:* "Twas brillig, and the slythy toves / Did gyre and gymble in the wabe."

'Twas brillig in Death Valley, all right, with the sun just about to start dropping behind the Panamint Mountains, and there was nary a slythy tove in sight. . . . Where, oh where, could they be?

BADWATER, GOOD BEER

— *Withanee* —

We started off into the heat waves for the last time. The walking on this little spot was wonderful; the salt creeks felt like a spongy carpet that was doing its best to keep me upright. My body was giving out, but my mind was laser focused. The guys on either side of me seemed to mirror my mental state and dare I say we were almost even enjoying ourselves, taking pictures and daydreaming about what it was going to feel like to finally be done with this thing. The sponginess soon hardened, giving way to cracked and crunchy salt. Each step sounded a little like walking through frozen snow. Still though, it wasn't bad going in comparison to what the soles of our shoes had seen in the last week.

We made our way toward the part of The Walk I was most worried about, what is known as "Devil's Golf Course," and for good reason. It got its name after a 1934 National Park Service guide book said, "Only the devil could play golf" on its surface. Shawn and I had driven out there with Mom and Dad a year earlier, and I had been to Death Valley many times, so I was very familiar with the phenomenon that is Devil's Golf Course. Josh had never seen it, so it was quite cute when he smiled at me and said, "Withy. This isn't as bad as you made it sound! We got this! Sandwalkers!"

Bless his heart. Shawn and I glanced over at each other and sadly Shawn explained, "Oh, brother. We aren't on it yet."

Maybe we were, technically. I'm not too sure. But the ground wasn't what we knew it would be, though the pretty lines running all sorts of directions on the cracked desert floor were starting to lift up, forming lips and ledges we were having to step over. Stepping over an inch-or-two line of salt every few seconds doesn't seem like a big deal now, but man, it hurt like the dickens to lift my leg even that little bit. It changed my gait from

Shadows of our former selves seem appropriate here.

the shuffling I had gotten so good at. This hurt considerably worse, but the pain at that point was relative. If I had to point to one of those doctor's smiley charts with the different levels of pain, mine would probably have been pushing a 9, with a sad orange smiley labeled "severe."

I always kind of figured I was in that pain boat alone, though looking back now I know that all three of us were getting tired. The guys were better at hiding it than I was, but to hear them tell it they were feeling it too. It had been a long and grueling week, and I think it started to show a little bit when we stumbled onto a small wooden post in some salt mounds. Less than a foot tall, it poked its little head out and Josh spotted it first. We were so far from where any normal human beings would be, so we puzzled over why it was there and what it meant. Josh's reasoning was that hey, that probably marks the lowest spot in elevation out here! And didn't that happen to be what we were trying to find?

Hmmmm.

Could be, and even though it wasn't marked in any way, we could think of no other reasonable explanation for it. The problem was, Shawn's map elevation didn't reflect that to be true, and this would go on to be a slight point of contention for the next few hours.

By Joshy's way of thinking then. . .wow, we had kind of *made it* to the lowest point from the highest. That would mean we could beeline it straight for the motor home that we could now see as a tiny white dot on the other side of Devil's Golf Course and start the celebrations. It just didn't make any sense though. From Shawn's map on his phone to the ones I had looked at before The Walk, I knew the lowest points were out in depths of Devil's Golf Course and in the Badwater Basin, neither of which we were standing in yet. We snapped a picture and kept walking, all the while I was ruminating on that stupid stick.

We moved on, trying to decide at which degree heading to go. Toward the motor home, where our growing support party was waiting? Or, toward what the map was showing as the lowest point in elevation in Devil's Golf Course. My personal struggle was raging inside of me, the possibility that I could finish this thing only to realize later that we didn't actually ever hit 282 feet below sea level had my stomach churning. I couldn't do that. I had to *know*, with some degree of certainty anyway, that we had done what we had set out to do. Otherwise, why did we put ourselves through this?!

I voiced my concerns, and I am pretty sure my sweet, kind, and loving older brother wanted to murder me and leave my body for the crows. Shawn leaned toward my way of thinking, maybe because he had to— I mean he was in this thing with me for life, so he probably knew better.

We turned our little mule train to the right, somewhat away from where the support party sat. It hurt my heart, but I just had to finish this thing properly, even if it (or my brother) killed me.

Josh's fortitude and physical strength had impressed me this week. Less than two weeks from being forty-one years old, his body and mind had run circles around mine. He and Shawn made perfect bookends for me during The Walk; while Shawn supported and often indulged my need for a little sympathy, a break, or warm backpack beers, Josh was on the other side pushing me to keep going and not quit, to dig deep, to fight for my dream. I always thought he would have made an excellent coach. The only time I had seen him show any sort of vulnerability in The Walk was his elevation sickness on Mt. Whitney and now, on the last day, on Devil's Golf Course.

By now we were in the thick of it. The ground had turned into huge, jagged pillars that were covered in an inch-or-two layer of rock-hard salt.

Devil's Golf Course is, indeed, hell.

If you reached down to touch the edges, they would cut you as easily as a glass edge and rub salt in your wound, literally. If the devil does indeed play golf, he was currently beating us over the head with his 7-iron. It was extremely slow going, and each step on top of one of those pinnacles was a chess move to the next. It required an incredible amount of balance, too, which is something our sore and broken bodies no longer had. Another fun element was that the pinnacles were 3 feet high in places, 1 foot in others, and on and on, with big gaps in between that were about the exact size of a tennis shoe. One misstep or loss of balance really could result in a nasty injury. I kept thinking, if one of these breaks off and my leg gets swallowed up but my body falls in the counter-direction, I could have a broken leg in addition to some salty cuts. This was sketchy in every sense of the word.

We hobbled around in a grid fashion for what seemed like an eternity. Shawn was watching his map, looking for that −282 feet. About fifteen or twenty minutes into this treacherous walking, Josh had spread himself out in front of us considerably. He was faster than I was, with those long legs of his, and the distance between us was growing. I am not sure how

Salt pinnacles of Devil's Golf Course.

much my brain made sense of what was happening, but I looked up in the distance for just a half second while I wobbled around trying to gain my balance on a pinnacle, jamming my trekking pole into the shallower part. My gaze found Josh, and I realized he was sitting. *Sitting.* On the razor blades of salt. I hollered out to see what he was doing, and how he answered is kind of a blur in my memory, but the point was he had fallen and skinned up his shin. Fortunately he was okay and just taking a minute. That must have hurt like heck, and I felt so bad—I mean he was out here because of me. He was going away from the motor home because of me. Oopsie. Sorry, brother.

At some point, we were all calling out to each other that we thought we had covered the lowest point in our grid. The moment was so unceremonious, and I was sorely disappointed not to see some sort of place marker with lettering that pinpointed the exact spot. Come on, Death Valley Park folks, get on that.

Finally, we shifted our gaze over to the Minnie Winnie in the distance. Though we had been able to see it for some time as we moved forward, it was not getting any bigger. I started to feel a little panicky. The second half of this day was taking hours longer than anyone had expected, and we were losing our light. We pivoted and started crunching across the pinnacles toward our support party. I was keeping in touch with them here and there on the radio, but now Dad came on, and I could sense in his voice that he was getting worried about the light too. What fool could survive this in the dark?! Well, that fool had. Because they ran out of water earlier than they had planned, the original guys had to make this trek across Devil's Golf Course in the pitch dark.

His was the exact situation I was hoping to avoid here, but the sun had slipped behind the mountains and the clock was ticking. Dad radioed that they could send someone out with flashlights if needed, but I told him to hang on for a bit longer. I don't know why I said that, but I tried to keep my voice happy and light during those transmissions. It was a lie. Not only had I bumped up to the full "10" frown on the doctor pain charts, I was stressed about how dark it was getting, and I was starting to get some ruffled feathers about Josh being so far in front of us. I started griping to Shawn, and he understood. He called out, "Hey, Josh! We have to finish this thing together, man; we are a team. Sandwalkers!"

As it turns out, Josh wasn't going to go running into the support party's arms and leave us to fend for ourselves out there, but he was so far ahead of me that I thought that might just be the case. He stopped to wait for Shawn and his gimp sister. A weird thing happened during those last 30 minutes or so. We should have easily been in full darkness at the rate we were moving, but I swear to you, God kept the light on for a little longer that day. We closed in on our support party, and I vividly remember my mom and aunt linking arms and doing the do-si-do, round and round. They cheered, they sang, they danced. We had commentary, one-liners, hollered interviews, maybe even a little bit of heckling. It was hilarious, and I would have laughed if I could have caught enough of my breath. These five loons brought us on home. At 6:43 p.m. on October 1, the Second Edition Sandwalkers stepped off of Devil's Golf Course and into the arms of their waiting support party. 131 miles and 7 days later, we had officially walked, or limped in my case, from the highest point in the contiguous United States to the lowest point in the Western Hemisphere.

I have since thought about this moment so many times. Whenever I feel like I can't accomplish something, whenever I feel like I'm not good enough, whenever I think I'm in pain, I dig into my mind and relive it,

It was all over but the drinkin'.

over and over again, until I feel tears tugging at my eyes and, somehow the rest of the world clears right on up.

I have not lived a remarkable life. I am not the one you will find jumping out of airplanes or adventuring around the world. I remember as a kid, I would marvel at all the stories my dad told me. He has done *so* many cool things, and once I thought, what story would I have to tell my kids? Not one that would interest them, that's for sure. The Walk changed all that. It changed everything. The person who stepped off those salt pinnacles that night wasn't the person who took that step through Whitney Portal. She wasn't even close.

I have not lived a remarkable life, that is true. I am, however, surrounded by remarkable people. As I looked around our circle, everything kind of went into slow motion and I somehow found the wherewithal to think to myself how grateful I was for each of them. I watched my future

A moment we will never forget.

husband hug my dad, the lights of my life, the two of them forever having the memory of asking for my hand in marriage. I watched the ground twirl around as my big brother lifted me high in the air and spun circles, both of us howling to the sky. I was engulfed by my teeny little mom who threw her arms around me and said, "I can't believe you did it, With!" I saw my aunt, uncle, and cousin, who had driven more than 6 hours just to sit and wait for us to show up, dancing and hooting and laughing and taking our pictures and bear hugging us. We cracked beers; we popped champagne; we guzzled straight from the bottle. I caught Shawn's eye, and it had that twinkle in it that I will never tire of. As he draped his arm over my shoulder and we limped our way back to our faithful Minnie Winnie, I thought to myself, "Every single step of those 131 miles was absolutely, unequivocally, without a doubt, worth it.

Ouch, *damnit.*

OF (DEVIL'S GOLF) COURSE!

— Jim —

Waiting at Devil's Golf Course for the Sandwalkers to show up was like waiting for an overdue airliner; what started out as slight unease turned progressively into concerns that were only kept in check by using a whack-a-mole technique on them. There was a time in my life, not all that long ago, when it seemed worry was my constant nagging companion. I wasn't about to let myself get back into that state, but...where on earth *were* they? We had five sets of eyeballs searching every nook and salt-cranny with no results at all until Roger said, "I see movement out there." He pointed toward an area I'd just checked with my binoculars so I checked it again. Roger, after all, had somehow noticed a huge iron gate in plain sight at Westside Road that was all but invisible to me. But again, nothing. I handed the binoculars to Roger who twisted the focus wheel and said, "That's them, right out there."

I sighted along his outstretched arm and sure enough, there was movement way, way out there in a direction I hadn't quite anticipated. They weren't as far south as I thought they'd be. And they weren't nearly as close as I thought they'd be, either. I found out later that Shawn had followed his GPS to where it showed a lowest point to be, so I couldn't argue with that. I mean, the guy had never been in the town of Lone Pine in his life either but had followed his little electronic gizmo right into Jake's Saloon, while on foot, yet. If it could find that it could certainly guide him to an unmarked location a lot better than our old USGS topographical maps could. That map had shown the nearest 282-feet-below-sea-level point to be out in the salt pinnacles about half a mile south of where Minnie Winnie was now parked. It was apparently not recognized by any sort of official marker, unless it was that small salt-encrusted post set in a slight depression out there. Back then we'd left our packs leaning against the sign at the parking lot and more or less staggered down to that unremarkable basin and had to settle for that to be the end of our trek. There was no absolute confirmation of the lowest point being at that particular spot, but it was all we had. Even still, we barely had enough energy left to get back to our packs, finishing up the last sips of water we had. I fervently hoped the Second Edition was faring better.

But as we watched the slowly approaching figures, the sun was touching the tops of the Panamint Mountains. It seemed impossible for them to get over to us before dark. They would probably be in need of good flashlights before reaching us, and we voted the youngest among us—"Gunner" by name—to go out there on this particular resupply mission if needed. To his credit he agreed without so much as a recount. I radioed Withanee with our plan and cautioned her not to get in a hurry, as the salt pinnacles were nothing to rush across. As if she didn't know, huh?

The sun sank behind the Panamints but—and here's the kicker—the twilight just hung there like Grandma's sheets on the clothesline. It sounds, and was, hard to believe. I took a series of pictures as the hikers came closer and closer with agonizing slowness, and the light just kept hanging there. It didn't fade out like it does after daylight ends, and I can't say as I've seen anything like it in, ahem...well, all my years.

I would later look at the properties of those photos that shows the time each was taken, which turned out to be mindboggling to say the least. The farthest (first in the series below) was snapped at 6:39 p.m. on October 1, 2017. There was then a series of three photos I took as they slowly closed in, each showing the *same* time of 6:43 p.m., and finally a photo taken—after much hugging and backslapping and dancing—of the three in the parking area toasting with champagne at 6:45 p.m. So the whole journey from when I snapped the first photo way across the salt pinnacles to the official toast took 6 minutes, in by-the-clock time. However, at least 40 to 50 minutes had to have gone by that we actually lived through. Go figure, huh? We'd just have to lump it in with Westside Road being open, the healing of Withy's nosebleed, and the smooth-running 4Runner after having apparently blown its little engine, among other improbable things. There are people who would argue we were obviously on the backroads of Rod Serling's *Twilight Zone,* but there are also those of us who recognize these occurrences as miracles wrought by the Author of *Basic Instructions Before Leaving Earth,* a volume otherwise known as the Bible.

The very slow progression of the Sandwalkers as they cross the finish line, and yet, total darkness didn't envelope them. Just one more miracle witnessed in the past week.

What a great reunion we had as darkness finally closed in, the Second Edition outfitted in their champagne-splashed shirts they so resolutely earned, the rest of us trying not to knock each other down in exuberant celebration of this awe-inspiring moment. I got all teary-eyed just being there. They did it. They actually climbed to the summit of Mt. Whitney and then turned around and walked 131 miles to Devil's Golf Course near Badwater. One must ask what kind of a nut would even consider doing something like that, for crying out loud.

THE BEST DARN TROPHY

— *Withanee* —

Dad, Josh, Shawn, Gunner, Uncle Roger, and I climbed into the Minnie Winnie, some more nimbly than others. Mom and Shell hopped in the Toyota and followed as we moved our celebration back to Furnace Creek. The ride was fun; we regaled our listeners with the second half of the day, and maybe drank a couple of beers as we cruised on down the highway. Maybe. I can't remember.

When we got in, I figured we would go to the bar for the rest of the night. I was in a mood to party like it was 1974, just like the OGs. God had better plans, though, and most everything in Furnace Creek was closed due to construction. The only place that was open was the restaurant on the golf course, which looked more like a warehouse, and it was pretty packed. We hobbled in and ordered up some pizzas and beers. We were filthy, tired, probably a little offensive odor-wise, but ecstatic. All still wearing our matching shirts, I will never forget a little old white-haired lady who ran up to us pointing and asking, "What on earth...is a Sand-walker!!?" Boy, did she get an answer.

After dinner we all went back to our wonderful room and relaxed. After our supporters left for the evening, Mom *promising* me that she would make me some French toast the next day to make up for the jambalaya incident, I took a shower and used a glorious blow dryer without a single light flicker. Ahhhh.

The next morning Josh, Shawn, and I were having a cup of coffee while watching the breaking news about the horrific shooting in Las Vegas the night before. While we had been celebrating the accomplishment of a lifetime, a shooter had opened fire on a crowd at a country concert from a nearby casino. There was something about that tragedy, coupled with the feat we had just experienced, that just gave me the chills. Made me almost grateful for all my aches and pains. Almost.

We met Mom, Dad, and crew at the Minnie Winnie at the RV park a couple miles down the road. As soon as I opened the door of the car, the smell of French toast filled my senses. There it is. That is exactly what got me up that mountain down on Wildrose. Thanks, Mom.

We all ate breakfast together at a picnic table, and it was wonderful, both the food and the company. After breakfast, Shawn handed Dad his book and said, "You've got one chapter left to read us, sir."

We gathered 'round as Dad read the final chapter of his book. Much of what he had penned was exactly what we had felt, and it really did tie a bow on the whole thing. While he was reading, Shawn was hunched over his walking stick, chuckling from time to time at the story. After Dad had finished, Shawn presented his project: he had scraped off six bare spots on that darn branch he had cut down at the base of Mt. Whitney and was now having the Second Edition Sandwalkers and support party sign each spot with a permanent marker. It felt like such an incredible honor to sign that silly stick. Once we got it home, he covered that thing in lacquer, and our trophy now sits on display in the very first home we have ever owned.

"IT AIN'T OVER 'TIL IT'S OVER"

—Jim—

This chapter's title is a direct quote from Yogi Berra, a twentieth-century baseball player for the New York Yankees known for mixing all kinds of metaphors and sayings into head-scratching verses, such as "Déjà vu all over again," but with this particular title he hit the nail on his head. See? That kind of stuff.

Anyway, we jumped into Minnie Winnie for the last time as a unit to ride back to Furnace Creek, where Val had thoughtfully provided rooms for the Sandwalkers so they wouldn't have to sleep outside on this singular occasion. Val volunteered to drive Yoda back, and if I was half as gallant as I hoped, I would have insisted she ride in the motor home while I brought up the rear in Yoda. But I didn't, because it never crossed my mind. Val had done the lion's share of the support work and should have enjoyed the fruits thereof on this final drive to Furnace Creek with all of them together, but I like to think my action of elbowing my way in was because I was too tired to be honorable. I try not to mull that over very often.

When we arrived at the campsite our walkers transferred their gear to Josh's Subaru and drove over to check into their rooms, followed by Roger, Michelle, and Gunner in Roger's rig, a crew-cab pickup suitable for his job at a gold mine. Val and I followed in Yoda after a quick cleaning of Minnie, all of us meeting at the temporary restaurant set up for tourists who were braving the construction shutdowns.

Furnace Creek Inn and Ranch had always been kind of a ritzy place that suggested a comfortable wild west—more cowboy boots than tuxedos, but uniquely American with class. It was pricey for us country folks but well worth it because (A) It was in the infamous Death Valley, and (B) It offered year-round warmth and relaxation amid awe-inspiring wonder. About 90 percent of it was now secreted behind an impenetrable 6-foot fence amongst the palm trees, while the escaping dust and noise revealed jackhammers and associated equipment at work. It was obviously a huge makeover. A sign informed us that the Furnace Creek Inn and Ranch was in the throes of becoming "The Oasis at Furnace Creek." I found that discombobulating, but I don't know why.

The temporary restaurant looked exactly like you'd expect a temporary restaurant to look: a large open dining area that wasn't quite plumb peppered with tables that didn't quite match bordered by what appeared to be homemade counters. It seemed awfully busy for a resort that was shut down at the moment, and as we stood inside the door studying the lay of the land a small white-haired old lady walked up and asked, right out of the blue, "What's a Sandwalker?"

That took us aback for a moment until one of us—I don't recall who—remembered we were wearing our custom Sandwalker shirts and took the time to nicely explain about the walk. She was duly impressed and so were we. What a warm, unexpected welcome that gave us.

We found a table that would seat the eight of us near the door and put together our order from the large whiteboard menu suspended above the "order here" counter. Some of us got up and went for food, which was mostly pizza and burgers, and some of us got up and went for drinks, which was mostly India Pale Ale. I didn't go anywhere because someone had to sit there and keep our table safe or something. I'm not one to toot my own horn, but I did a fine job of that and everything was still A-OK when they returned.

I don't remember much about our meal, and I don't believe anybody else does either, mainly because we were actually and genuinely and really, *really* done with The Walk. I don't think any of us could quite come to grips with that. I'm sure I had the same feeling forty-three years ago, but I hadn't gotten it out and dusted it off since then. The surreal loop that had been hovering around my pea brain for the past week was now complete, and I couldn't stop staring at my daughter. What a girl. I was deeply honored that she thought enough of her dad that she would even entertain the thought of recreating that grueling walk, let alone actually repeating it.

The Walk spoke volumes about the character and toughness of all three of the Second Edition; if they were fortunate enough to average twenty-four inches of ground with every step they took it comes out to 345,840 steps—not counting the initial hike up Whitney—of which the only easy steps were the first and the last. In between they spanned what the *Oakland Tribune* once described as "some of the roughest and most forbidding terrain on the continent." It's a wonder any of us made it. By "any of us" I include Glenn Burnett, Gary Ivie, and Ken Oberg, the missing OG Sandwalkers from 1974. It was somehow fitting that the new generation of Sandwalkers seated at the table this night were numbered at three.

But there we sat, surrounded by loving family, sharing pizza and beer and good times, which had become really good times when seen through the rear-view mirror. It doesn't get much better than that.

We broke up early as weariness was setting in on everybody, and after a group hug they headed for their rooms while Val drove me back to the campground in Yoda. Val. On top of everything else she's always the cheerful designated driver, and as a rule of thumb, I believe it would be foolish to try something of this magnitude if you don't have a Val around somewhere.

The following morning we tried to sleep in but couldn't, I suppose, because we hadn't woken up to daylight since we got Minnie. Val had promised Withy she'd make French toast this morning but since there were going to be eight for breakfast we found we were going to have to come up with more bread, somehow. With no store within an hour's drive that could be a problem. Val did some delegating and phoned over to the rooms to see if any of our entourage could come up with a loaf of bread over there. Sure enough, when they arrived at the campground Roger handed over a loaf he found at a bare-bones mini/micro store apparently set up for desperate guests such as ourselves. That guy comes in handy at times.

We had our French toast and coffee seated at one of those ubiquitous wooden tables you see scattered around every campground in America, after which I allowed my modest self to be cajoled into reading the final chapter of my book. I thought that would finally bring the curtain down on our adventure, but Shawn had one more waiting in the wings. He brought out his handmade walking stick that he'd fashioned from a pine limb back at Mt. Whitney, and after whittling six elongated sections down to bare wood he had all of us involved in the Walk sign our names for posterity. Val and I had the honor of signing first, which was a nice touch, followed by Josh and Withanee and Shawn himself. The sixth spot was left blank for honorary Sandwalker Kelly Harper to sign. She could only get enough time off work to climb Mt. Whitney, but she did that so well she secured herself a spot on Shawn's walking stick. Too bad she couldn't have finished the whole trip; she missed out on some great French toast.

And then, just like the chapter title suggests, the Walk of Ages part that was over, was over.

EPILOGUE

— Withanee —

Post-walk life tried to resume to normal, but as I said before, nothing was ever normal again. We all went back to our respective cities and for about a month every time I got into bed, I was overcome with homesickness for my sleeping bag next to the Minnie Winnie, under the stars.

Five months later, Josh moved away to Texas to be with his girlfriend. Boy do I miss him. I'll always be so grateful that he went on that journey with me. Back when I first got this hare-brained idea, Josh was the first person I thought to invite along. He didn't pause or stutter whatsoever; he was with me from the very start. As he tells it, he went along to make sure I didn't quit. And man, did he hold up to that promise.

Shawn and I went back to our little cabin in South Lake Tahoe and started dabbling in wedding plans. I am not positive, but I think he could feel the change after The Walk, too. We had been through something together that tested us, day after day, much like marriage does. We not only had survived, we had thrived. Well, kind of. He gave me the proposal of a lifetime and has continued to treat me like he did every day of that week we were out there—supportive, loving, doing things that make me howl with laughter, handing me a beer after a bad day. As I see it, it just doesn't get any better.

Mom and Dad had the tedious task of taking the rented RV back all the way to Kingman, Arizona, where they had gotten it. Of course, they gave it a darn good scrubbing first, and the folks they rented it from said they had never seen it so clean. A support party's work is never done, I suppose. Mom had worked her tail off that week, and I am so grateful for her. We talk every single day, so, I guess a parent's support job really never *is* done.

That brings me to my father. I still can't believe that man. How he made that walk forty-three years before I did, without technology, without having ever done anything really physical, without a Minnie Winnie *for crying out loud,* having come from living around sea level to 14,508 feet without any acclimation, all while smoking cigarettes. . . . I mean, come on. It's incredible. We had so many more comforts than he did, but the biggest one of all was that we got to tote around our very own OG Sandwalker. Someone who could line us out each night for what we could expect the next day, who knew exactly how much pain we felt, who guided us through the ins and outs of this club of seven we were now a part of forever. Wow.

I did this walk to honor my dad. I wanted to walk, or limp, in his footsteps, and I did in every way possible. It's funny, you know, how everything between his journey and mine paralleled almost exactly. He blew his right knee coming down Whitney and so did I—I still wear a brace when I work out. We faced the same battles—always brought up the back of the pack, both found a way to break through the wall with our famous high kick-step combo, both ran out of water before Westside Road on the last day, both got a stubborn hold of pushing forward to the very last −282 feet when temptations told us otherwise. As painful as it was, The Walk was the best week of my life. Spending each night with my parents, brother, and now-husband, laughing and listening to Dad read, being woken up by serenade, and seeing them parked and waiting for us in the distance are memories that I will carry with me for the rest of my life. I am forever better for it.

Because of the void I felt after it was all over, I decided that I would do one "epic" thing per year. I guess I am still searching for that same incredible high I got at the end of The Walk, and though I know it may never be as intense, I guess I will no longer live my life in mediocrity. So far, I've gotten hitched, traveled out of the country, ran a half marathon, bought a house, and the biggest one yet: written a book with my best friend, my dad.

EPILOGUE

—Jim—

"ep·i·logue : noun: a section at the end of a book that serves as a comment on or a conclusion to what has happened"

Well, OK. My first comment is about my daughter's name, *Withanee;* my last name is Andersen, so I'm always explaining that there is no "o" in there. My father's side was from Norway, and they spelled Andersen wrong, apparently. So my constant explanation growing up was, "It's Andersen, spelled with an 'e.'" Hence my daughter's name *Withanee.* I had to add another e to the end of it so people wouldn't pronounce it "With-*ain*." No. "With-an-*ee*" it is, and although she very much disliked it early on she has since taken to it like a duck to water. Her married name now though is Milligan, with an "a." This proves that planning was never my strong suit, even before The Walk.

I say all this because I'm following what Withanee did in writing this book. She has a degree in journalism from the University of Nevada, Reno, so she knows about this stuff, and since she felt compelled to follow in my footsteps across that vast, unfriendly land between Mt. Whitney and Death Valley I thought it only fair that I follow her lead throughout this more cerebral but no less difficult work of a sequel, and because she ended this book with an epilogue, well. . . .

After all, fair is fair.

So my first real comment on what has happened involves the disparity of recorded mileages; our original walk was pegged at 143 miles, while this recent one tallied 131 miles. The Second Edition certainly shaved off a portion of mileage by their use of GPS which I believe can account for at least half of the twelve-mile difference, maybe more. The remainder can

The Original Sandwalkers of 1974. I'm on the far left, struggling to stay upright. Like father like daughter, eh?

be explained, in my unenlightened opinion, by the original Sandwalkers use of the cutting-edge hiking odometer aptly named a "pedometer." It's a little gadget that looks like a pocket watch topped with a belt clip that, of course, clips to your belt. By positioning it directly in front of one leg it records distance by means of the pendulum-swinging motion whenever you take a step. The bugaboo here is that you must dial in the correct distance, in inches, of one of your steps in order to come up with an accurate account of mileage traveled. GIGO, which would later become the watchword of computerese, was relevant in the distance setting of the pedometer: you put garbage in, you get garbage out, and although I kept dialing down the inches as blisters and aches shortened my steps, it was mostly guesswork. And I wouldn't be at all surprised if that pedometer didn't bounce in a couple of extra miles just crossing the salt pinnacles that horrible night.

You can view the pedometer in the picture of the four of us original Sandwalkers all dressed in white on Emigrant Gap, just prior to climbing down into Death Valley proper. I'm on the far left and the pedometer hangs like a pocketwatch off the front of my belt.

Considering the differences in hardware we had in relation to the Second Edition, I'm actually pleasantly surprised that our mileages came to be as close as they were.

Another thing that causes one to scratch one's head is the elevation of Mt. Whitney. When we originally summitted we were met with a bronze plaque affixed to a boulder that proclaimed its height as 14,495.811 feet above sea level. That is truly amazing on the face of it: not 14,496, but 14,495.*811*. That is bringing the measurement down to the thousandths of a foot. Machinists work with thousandths, but I wasn't aware that surveyors did also, especially back in 1930. Perhaps we haven't come as far as we thought, mathematically speaking, for the official elevation of Mt. Whitney today is 14,505 feet. Apparently the surveyors of 1930 were off by nine and one-hundred-eighty-nine thousandths of a foot, or our modern surveyors erred, or the mountain grew that much. And here's another wrinkle: when the Second Edition summited in 2017 there was a professional-looking wooden sign up there suitable for photo ops that gave the elevation as 14,508 feet.

However it pans out, though, it would appear that the Second Edition Sandwalkers have taken over the highest point in the highest-to-lowest competition by at least 9.189 feet. But us OGs still own the rest, at least if Death Valley has indeed remained at 282 feet below sea level.

As for the crew themselves Withanee has brought most everything up to date in her epilogue, so I won't get into any of that other than to say that after spending that time with them, in those most demanding and grueling of conditions, I'm convinced they represent the very finest of their generation in every respect, and that their generation is every bit as tough and proud and as imbued with American stick-to-itiveness as ours was.

And lastly, this note on the original Sandwalkers: right after we returned to our jobs at the paper mill in Antioch, California, we lost contact, mainly because I quit my job as a maintenance welder and moved to a small town in Nevada. I never again saw Gary Ivie, and I only saw Glenn and Ken one time each. Ken visited with some of the millworkers a couple years after I moved, and I saw Glenn once after the turn of the century when he was driving through. But I tried for thirty years to find out where they had all got off to—the paper mill shut down not too long after The Walk—without success. Even after computers came along I couldn't find them, nor could any of my computer-savvy friends.

On the day we completed our trek, one of the four of us noticed that in the year 1999 (wow, that was so far in the future as to be almost unthinkable!) it would be exactly twenty-five years since we finished The Walk, and in a fit of sentimentalism we agreed to meet at Devil's Golf Course on June 23 to celebrate the twenty-fifth anniversary. That didn't exactly pan out, as I discovered when I stood there on that date in 1999. Val and I waited for an hour or so and then gave up when nobody showed. We also checked at Furnace Creek, Stovepipe Wells, Lone Pine, and Whitney Portal. Nothing, zip, nada.

The year after The Walk, Withanee somehow tracked down every one of the old Sandwalkers and was able to give me their phone numbers and addresses. She talked with each one first, mainly to make sure they were the right ones, and they were amazed that another generation had joined the sandwalking ranks. I was able to talk to each one again after so long, but since I forgot to ask about the reunion, apparently it had now been forgotten by all of us. They were old men now, so that shouldn't have been surprising in their case. What was more surprising was that we didn't seem to have much to talk about after maybe fifteen minutes. It sure doesn't take long to bring old friends up to date. We invited all of them to Shawn and Withanee's wedding in Nevada City, and Ken actually showed up with his wife. We had a wonderful reunion, in the manner of which cannot be done over the phone. I sent them all a copy of my book on our walk though.

Original Sandwalkers, 1974, and Second Edition Sandwalkers, 2017

Sadly, last year both Gary Ivie and Ken Oberg passed away, and it surprised me that after all that time I felt so much grief, but then I'm sure we bonded more than any of us realized on that journey. May they rest in peace.

And, for the last comment, I just have to relate an interesting thing that took place in 1999 when Val and I attempted that reunion thing; at Whitney Portal Val started up the Mt. Whitney Trail. You weren't supposed to do that without a permit, but surely she'd turn back after taking a couple pictures, right?

Wrong. She kept going and going and going, up switchbacks and through creeks all the way to Lone Pine Lake, me all the while chasing behind saying "Stop, go back, stop, go back, huff-puff." I was toting one of those big shoulder-mounted VHS cameras about the size you see at NFL games, so I got a lot of it on tape, but man was I tired. And although I was worried we were going to get caught, all the while I was thinking where was she when I did this the first time?

We finally turned around at the lake, but I think that day was the reason she so badly wanted to walk with the Second Edition on their trip. And you know something? She would have made it.

One can only hope that isn't the start of another one of these things.

POSTSCRIPT

— *Withanee* —

At the time we completed The Walk, I knew I had done something truly special, something that somehow furthered an already unbreakable bond with my father. Yet, with the turning pages of time, this particular week of our lives has become even more significant than I ever imagined.

My sweet, hilarious, loving, incredible, sandwalking Dad went home to be with the Lord on May 12, 2022. He was *so* excited about the prospect of our story (mixed with a little love, adventure, and IPA) becoming a book and we dreamed about that for a long time. We spent countless hours pouring over these pages together, laughing, wincing, rewriting, smiling, remembering. They live and breathe with exactly who he was, his sense of purpose in life and his unyielding faith.

Of course, the only reason this journey meant anything at all was because of my dad. I could never aptly put into words what he means to me, but recreating such an important part of his life perhaps spoke to him better than I ever could. As it turns out, The Walk was simply a metaphor for our lives. His role as "support party" is exactly what he has been in my life since the day I was born. The journey is exactly as life is itself: painful, yet incredibly rewarding when you surround yourself with the right people. I also want to mention that we spread some of my dad's ashes in Alabama Hills at the base of Mt. Whitney. That way, he can continue to keep an eye on that cantankerous old mountain. I don't know if he would laugh or slap us upside the head. Knowing him, probably both.

This journey wasn't confined to the week we made it, or even the week my dad made it back in '74. I've thought about it every day since, and it has given me the incredible gift of precious memories and time—the only commodities that matter. I can still feel the overflowing love of my

I love you, Dad.

dad wrapping me up in his arms each night as we came limping into camp. I can hear his voice—encouraging, laughing, reading us the next day's chapter, singing Creedence. I can see his bright blue eyes fill with tears when he stares at Shawn and I, or watches our engagement video on repeat. I can feel the overwhelming joy of seeing him tootling down the road toward me in the Minnie Winnie. I can picture the pride on his face, perhaps with a dash of shock, when we cross the finish line. I often pull these memories over me like a blanket when the world feels as jagged as the pinnacles of Devil's Golf Course. And somehow, they ease the sting every single time.

Looking back now, I more clearly understand the point of it all, and man, was it worth it. Much like The Walk itself, this book was yet another dream of ours that came true.

We truly thank you for coming along for the ride. Or, you know, *walk*.

ABOUT THE AUTHORS

WITHANEE ANDERSEN earned her bachelor's degree from the Reynold's School of Journalism at the University of Nevada, Reno. Her first published article was included in *Sagebrushed: Coming of Age and Working in Nevada.* She was a wildland firefighter for many years, a marketing specialist for a destination management organization, and is now the Communications Coordinator for the City of Sparks, where she uses her storytelling and copyediting skills daily.

JIM ANDERSEN (1944–2022) was a freelance writer whose career began in 1980 with *Nevada Magazine.* He also wrote for the *Battle Mountain Bugle* and the *Reese River Reveille.* In 2005, he received first place from the Nevada Press Association for the "Best Local Non-Staff Column." He is the author of *Lost in Austin: A Nevada Memoir* and *Sometimes a Great Notion...isn't, so much.* This book is his final work.